FLAMING SOULS

Homosexuality, Homophobia, and Social Change in
Barbados

While there has been increased attention to issues of sexuality in the Caribbean over the past decade, there continue to be very few in-depth ethnographic
studies of sexual minorities in this region. A timely addition to the literature,
Flaming Souls explores public discourses focusing on homosexuality and the
everyday lives of gay men and 'queens' in contemporary Barbados.

David A.B. Murray's dynamic study features interviews with government
and health agency officials, HIV/AIDS activists, and residents of the country's
capital, Bridgetown. Using these and records from local libraries and archives,
Murray unravels the complex historical, social, political, and economic forces
through which same-sex desire, identity, and prejudice are produced and valued
in this Caribbean nation-state. Illustrating the influence of both Euro-American and regional gender and sexual politics on sexual diversity in Barbados,
Flaming Souls makes an important contribution to queer studies and the
anthropology of sexualities.

DAVID A.B. MURRAY is an associate professor of Anthropology and member of
the Sexuality Studies Program at York University.

Flaming Souls

*Homosexuality, Homophobia,
and Social Change in Barbados*

DAVID A.B. MURRAY

UNIVERSITY OF TORONTO PRESS
Toronto Buffalo London

© University of Toronto Press 2012
Toronto Buffalo London
www.utppublishing.com
Printed in Canada

ISBN 978-1-4426-4448-9 (cloth)
ISBN 978-1-4426-1300-3 (paper)

∞

Printed on acid-free, 100% post-consumer recycled paper with vegetable-based inks.

Library and Archives Canada Cataloguing in Publication

Murray, David A. B., 1962–
Flaming souls : homosexuality, homophobia, and social change in Barbados / David A.B. Murray.

Includes bibliographical references and index.
ISBN 978-1-4426-4448-9 (bound). – ISBN 978-1-4426-1300-3 (pbk.)

1. Homosexuality – Social aspects – Barbados. 2. Homophobia – Barbados. 3. Gay rights – Barbados. 4. Gay men – Barbados – Social conditions. I. Title.

HQ76.3.B3M87 2012   306.76′60972981   C2011-908279-9

This book has been published with the help of a grant from the Canadian Federation for the Humanities and Social Sciences, through the Aid to Scholarly Publications Program, using funds provided by the Social Sciences and Humanities Research Council of Canada.

University of Toronto Press acknowledges the financial assistance to its publishing program of the Canada Council for the Arts and the Ontario Arts Council.

 Canada Council   Conseil des Arts
for the Arts   du Canada

 ONTARIO ARTS COUNCIL
CONSEIL DES ARTS DE L'ONTARIO

University of Toronto Press acknowledges the financial support of the Government of Canada through the Canada Book Fund for its publishing activities.

In loving memory of Al

Contents

Acknowledgments

It is difficult to know where to begin to thank all the individuals, groups, and institutions who have given me so much of their time, wisdom, patience, and resources over the ten years that I have been working on this project. While I have tried to keep lists of those who have provided assistance and support, I apologize in advance to those whom I forget to mention in the following paragraphs and ask them to forgive me and my increasingly forgetful mind.

I would not have been able to write a word of this book without 'Joyce,' my friend and confidante for over fifteen years. It was Joyce who let me stay with her during my first trip to Barbados, who, over subsequent years, introduced me to her family, friends, and neighbours, and who patiently, very patiently, answered my ill-formed questions and tried to clarify my many misunderstandings of conversations and encounters. Darcy Dear, founder and president of United Gays and Lesbians Against Aids in Barbados (UGLAAB) has also been incredibly supportive, kind, and helpful over many years, not only offering me his precious time and deep knowledge but also introducing me to fellow queens, friends, and colleagues. There are numerous other members of UGLAAB and a number of individuals – Didi Winston, 'Divina,' 'Cherry,' 'Mr Lovelace,' 'Omar,' 'Gigi,' 'Cynthia,' 'Michael,' and 'Tony' – who have also been very generous with their time and knowledge; once again, this book would not exist without their contributions.

In 2004–5, I had the privilege of being a visiting faculty member at the Sir Arthur Lewis Institute for Social and Economic Studies at the University of the West Indies, Cave Hill campus. I would like to thank Professor Andrew Downes, his staff, and the resident faculty members of the institute for their gracious hospitality and support. In particular, I would like to thank the institute's librarian, Ms Beverly Hinds, for her assistance in finding numerous texts and articles, as well as for her humorous and thoughtful insights into Bajan society. While at the University of West Indies, I met a number of faculty members who stimulated new ideas and rigorously critiqued existing ones; they include Tracy Robinson, Marcia Burrowes, Christine Barrow, and Joan Cuffie. Last, but not least, while in Barbados I was fortunate enough to meet and become friends with Andy Taitt, whose generosity, knowledge of all things Bajan, and excellent fish stew have been invaluable to me.

My writing and thinking have been enriched through the conversations with and assistance and feedback from friends, colleagues, and students at York University and other universities, including Kamala Kempadoo, Andil Gosine, Michelle Johnson, Andrea Davis, Alissa Trotz, Melanie Newton, Rinaldo Walcott, Winston Husbands, Clemon George, Thomas Glave, Kamari Clarke, Anne Meneley, Robert Carr, Aaron Kamugisha, Charmaine Crawford, Fatimah Jackson, Jillian Ollivierre, Karen McGarry, Danielle Bryant, Caglayan Ayan, and Salman Hussain. I am very grateful to all of them for their support and critical engagement of the issues through which I am trying to work in this book. A final thank you goes to Ewan Atkinson (www.ewanatkinson.com) for allowing me to include his artwork on the cover.

Major funding for this research was provided by a Social Sciences and Humanities Research Council of Canada standard research grant and York University Faculty of Arts research grants. Previous sections of this manuscript have been published in the following journals: *Journal of Culture Health and Sexuality* (chapter 2), *Caribbean Review of Gender Studies* (chapter 5), and *Sexualities* (chapter 4). A shorter version of chapter 1 was previously published in my edited volume *Homophobias: Lust and Loathing across Time and Space* (Duke University Press, 2009). Needless to say, the opinions and arguments expressed in the following pages are my own and do not necessarily reflect those of my interlocutors.

FLAMING SOULS

Introduction

> Let's talk about the men.
> The green ones. They've taken
> The fire. Stole away from Dad's
> Mountain to the unspeakable mystery
> Of the Disco. The mystery of man on the
> Beast. And if this is Babylon and the fire awaits
> Then trap it. The heat of their flaming souls
> In Revelations. Green now. Different now. Abomination
> That thing of beauty. Where climax feeds on the riddles
> Of Disco's lusty lyric. Trap
> Them.
>
> Excerpt from 'Surrender' by Faizal Deen (Glave 2008)

In recent years, across much of the global North, lesbian, gay, bisexual, and transgender (LGBT) community events and activist groups have shifted their focus from local to global rights for sexual minorities, and this focus is now being taken up and supported by influential non-governmental human rights organizations; they in turn are pressuring governments and international agencies like the United Nations to revise their policies, laws, and/or legislation to support the rights of sexual minorities. In these events, discussions, and documents the Caribbean often appears as an example of one of the 'problem regions' that require attention and action. Following are a few recent events that focused on global sexual rights.

'Global human rights for queers' was a major theme in 2009 of Pride, a week of parades, exhibits, parties, and talks that takes place annually in Toronto, Canada, reflecting a 'collaborative effort between a wide range of diverse

LGBTTIQQ2S communities.'[1] The Pride parade, the biggest event of the week, is led by an international grand marshal along with the (local) grand marshal. The 2009 international grand marshal was Victor Juliet Makasa, a global trans-rights activist from Uganda, whose presence, Pride organizers declared, would allow 'us ... [to] pay tribute to the brave queer activists fighting for their rights in Africa and specifically in Uganda.'[2] In 2008 the international grand marshal was *Gareth Henry*, former co-chair of *Jamaica* Forum for Lesbians, All Sexuals, and Gays (JFLAG).

A few weeks later the second World Outgames in Copenhagen began with the second International Conference on LGBT Human Rights, whose theme was 'Love of Freedom – Freedom to Love.' The conference program stated that the overall goal of the conference was to 'reaffirm and defend the human rights of every LGBT person in the world to participate fully, equally, and openly in every part of life.' It included workshops that would help people learn to use 'political, legal, and other measures to work towards a world where all people, regardless of sexual orientation or gender identity, can live, love, and celebrate their identities with equal dignity and respect.'[3] The program website highlighted the fact that the keynote speakers were people who were fighting for LGBT rights 'around the world' and came from Latvia, the United States, *Jamaica, Trinidad,* Kenya, Lebanon, Brazil, and India.

The focus on rights for queers and on fighting homophobia around the world is not just the stuff of Pride parades and gay-games conferences. International human rights organizations like Human Rights Watch (HRW) and Amnesty International are now actively organizing campaigns to fight discrimination against queers and are writing reports that document violence against sexual minorities, with a particular focus on the global South, in which Caribbean countries once again figure prominently: In 2009, HRW published the report 'Together, Apart: Organization around Sexual Orientation and Gender Identity,' which argued that 'many groups defending LGBT rights – especially throughout the global South – still have limited access to funding, and courageously face sometimes murderous attacks without adequate support from a broader human rights community.'[4] The report provided brief overviews of sexual rights activism and gender and sexual minority movements in every region of the world. The Caribbean region was considered to be one of the most problematic areas. Previously, in 2004, HRW had published another report, entitled 'Hated to Death: Homophobia, Violence, and Jamaica's HIV/AIDS Epidemic,' which documented the everyday violence and discrimination against men who have or are perceived to have sex with men in that country.

Finally, at the Glasgow Gallery of Modern Art a 2009 exhibition, *SH(OUT): Contemporary Art and Human Rights*, contained a room dedicated to Amnesty

International's work to support people who are persecuted on the basis of their sexual or gender orientation around the world. The room contained photographs of people in different parts of the world, marching together and carrying rainbow flags and placards with statements like 'Love Is a Human Right.' One of the Amnesty International brochures available for patrons to take home contained a map documenting 'homophobia around the world' in 2008; twelve countries, including Jamaica, the United States, Poland, Morocco, and Nigeria, were highlighted.

Perhaps these documents and events help to explain why it was that in conversations with colleagues, family, and friends during the late 1990s and the first decade of the new millennium about my travel plans to the Caribbean (where I have been doing research since 1991), I was increasingly asked if the country to which I was travelling was 'gay friendly' or 'homophobic.' Or, conversely, I would be advised to 'be careful down there' because the person had heard or read about how homophobic 'that area' was. Another example of this increased 'awareness' of homophobia in the Caribbean could be found in the travel sections of North American mainstream newspapers, which contained bylines such as, 'While the Caribbean lags behind most of the western world in terms of openness toward gay visitors, signs of change are coming into view' (*Miami Herald* 2007).

Of course, when a region is labelled *homophobic*, it is the people of that region who are being identified as such. What struck me was the way in which this term was increasingly being used as a sociocultural trait or, more accurately, a pathological sociocultural trait, in which a group of (Caribbean) people's sexual attitudes were being judged and in which the (Euro-American) speaker's socio-sexual culture, place, or nation was being generally compared favourably (implicitly or explicitly) to that of the 'other' culture, place, or nation. Homophobia, in other words, was no longer something attributed to individuals or institutions in one's home community or society. Homophobia had gone global, and to be accused of being homophobic was to be accused of something more than disliking homosexuals; furthermore, this accusation now carried potentially serious economic and political repercussions for these places, cultures, or nations that were found 'guilty' of such discriminatory practices.

The increasing circulation of statements about the Caribbean as a homophobic region led me to wonder about the effects of utilizing homophobia as a sociocultural trait or pathology that is increasingly attached to the moral, political, and economic agendas of governments, development agencies, and human rights organizations. I also started to wonder about the meaning and existence of homophobia itself: What exactly is it? How and why does it exist in the first place? Is it problematic to speak of groups, communities, regions, or nations as homophobic? Who is privileged and who is silenced in such a claim? Is homophobia a universal prejudice that operates along identical axes of difference and power, or does it operate differently across diverse social, political, and economic terrains? If so, then how is it located in and generated in and through these terrains? More specifically, has there always been homophobia in the Caribbean? Might it be problematic to use this term to represent and analyse sexual difference and discrimination in the Caribbean? How do we go about researching the veracity of these kinds of claims? If forms of sexual inequality exist in Caribbean societies, where do they come from? Who or what produces them? Who challenges them, and how do they propose to eliminate them? What is life like for those who are the targets homophobic discourses? Do they perceive their societies to be homophobic? Do they view themselves as gay or queer victims?

This book represents my engagement with these questions. I focus on Barbados, an independent nation state with an estimated population of 276,302 as at the end of 2010,[5] which, according to some Bajans (a local term for Barbadian citizens) is 90 per cent gay, while others claim it is 100 per cent homophobic. These are claims that I heard not only from Bajans but also from other Caribbean people of different sexual orientations living in Canada and the United States and throughout the English- and French-speaking Caribbean. While living in Washington, DC, in the early 1990s, I dated a man from Barbados and became good friends with his sister Joyce, who lives in Bridgetown (the capital of Barbados) and would come up to Washington regularly to visit him. Amongst their Bajan friends (who, it should be noted, were mostly Barbadian women and gay-identified men) I heard many lively discussions and debates over how many Barbadian males were 'bullers' or gay and how receptive the rest of the island was to this group. As the reports of homophobia in the Caribbean became more vociferous and public during the 1990s and the first decade of the new millennium, with much of the attention focused on Jamaica (that is, debates over the homophobic lyrics of dance-hall music, and reports of a series of brutal attacks on gay men), I became increasingly curious about this other English-speaking, post-colonial, Caribbean nation state. Was Barbados, as some claimed, 'a gay-friendly' haven or was it, as others put it, 'a living hell' for anyone perceived to be homosexual? At the very least, the reports and condemnation by news and human rights agencies of uniform and aggressive homophobia in this region did not gel with the informal talk of these groups. I had lived and worked in Martinique (an overseas department of France that is located a few islands away from Barbados) on and off for a period of six years, from 1992 to 1998, and found that heteropatriarchy – the systemic, institutionalized privilege of a particular political-economic system of masculine hetero-sexuality – structured much public and popular culture. It made life difficult for many '*gai*' men there, some of whom told me that they dreamed of moving to a place like Quebec where, they had heard, there was less racism and homo-phobia than in Martinique or France (Murray 2002). My understanding of het-eropatriarchy in Martinique was deeply influenced by M. Jacqui Alexander's analysis that connects sexual politics to economic and political processes in the Bahamas and that foregrounds the way in which the Bahamian nation state consolidated a form of neo-imperial heteropatriarchal power through its laws, economic policies, and transnational political-economic alliances (Alexander 1994, 1997, 2005). But was it possible that Barbados might be notably dif-ferent from other English- and French-speaking Caribbean nations or depart-ments in terms of beliefs, attitudes, and values pertaining to gender and sexual diversity? Was the Barbadian state supportive or, at least, neutral in its poli-cies and practices pertaining to sexual minorities? Was heteropatriarchy less entrenched in popular and public discourses and institutions, and, if so, why? Were communities and neighbourhoods more tolerant of sexual diversity? Did queer people live more openly and freely in their day-to-day lives?

While it might be tempting to employ a quantitative research methodology to answer some of these questions (for example, how many homosexuals are there in Barbados? Exactly what proportion of the population is homosexual or homophobic?), my objective in the following chapters is not to establish or prove that one set of figures is right or wrong. In fact, one of the goals of this book is to question the frames of reference that are used to create these figures in the first place. No percentage really helps us understand how sexual desires, experiences, identities, and prejudices are organized, related, performed, and circulated in this nation state (or anywhere else, for that matter). My goal, therefore, is not to prove any statement about 'Barbadian (homo)sexuality' or 'Barbadian sexual attitudes' to be true or false; rather, I attempt to unravel some of the complex historical, social, political, and economic terrains through which desire, identification, belonging, difference, and power are produced, performed, evaluated, and ranked. In order to accomplish this task, I move through the different sites in Barbados – textual, electronic, and geographic – in which I saw, met, or heard someone, or read something, referring to gays or homosexuals. As we shall see, during the period in which I conducted this research (2002–8) I found no shortage of references to this topic in Barbadian public domains, from newspapers, radio call-in shows, and theatre perform-ances to government reports, parliamentary debates, and health-care discussions. Indeed there was a veritable kaleidoscope of individuals, groups, organizations, and institutions in Barbados opining on some aspect of 'the homosexual.'

Perhaps this should not be surprising. As any Foucault primer would tell you, the incitement to discourse produces a discursive explosion of knowledge, – in this case, about a particular formation of sexuality. These discourses have continually worked towards the normalization of sexuality (an impossible goal, Foucault argues) and have simultaneously created 'non-normative' sexualities and the need to cure, eradicate, or discipline them (Foucault 1978). One of Foucault's most important contributions to the analysis of the truth regime of sexuality was his argument about the way in which its power operates through multiple circuits simultaneously. However, many critics of Foucault have since noted numerous limitations to the scope of his enquiry. Foucault situated the formation of the discourses of sexuality primarily within the Western historical context of medical science and did not, in any sustained manner, interrogate how sexuality has also been produced in and through the organization and regulation of other social, political, and economic structures of inequality (class, race, gender) arising from the vast, powerful rubrics of colonialism, nationalism, and/or globalization (Garber 2003,127; Lyons and Lyons 2004, 13–15).

Taking Foucault and his critics into account, I argue that there is no one site or text in which *the* truth about Barbadian (or any other) sexuality can be found. Rather, we find a dense proliferation of discourses circulating through spaces and surfaces that are public, private, virtual, topographical, textual, corporeal, electronic, and/or archival. By employing a multi-sited approach that applies different methodological tools – discourse analysis, participant observation, and interviews – I hope to be able to demonstrate that sexuality, in particular homosexuality, is a productive metaphor, a simultaneously empty and overstuffed conceptual container through which social, political, and economic differences, formations, relations, and changes on micro and macro scales are rendered sensible or, conversely, threatened to be rendered insensible (see chapters 1 to 3). Put in slightly different terms, I argue that the homosexual is simultaneously central and marginal to the formation of the imagined[6] socio-political space known as Barbados – *central* in that his[7] presence throughout the diverse realms of Barbadian public life, from local newspapers and church pulpits to school boards, Ministry of Health publications, and parliamentary debates, illustrates the discursive power of a particular socio-sexual figure in relation to the perceived social, political, economic, physical, and moral health of all Barbadians; and *marginal* in that when these discussions, debates, and reports are read closely, we begin to see that while the homosexual may be the primary signifier, what is being signified is much more than just a position on a sexual identity. Rather, public discussions about the homosexual also (and always) invoke a host of other issues pertaining to identity, society, nation, economy, or other forms of social inequality. In other words, talk about homosexuality in Barbados (or anywhere else, for that matter) is rarely, if ever, just about the homosexual; it is a discourse, container, or rubric through which political, economic, gendered, racial, religious, and other forms of social difference, produced in and through the confluence of colonial histories and contemporary neo-liberal imperialisms, are organized, related, and situated (Puar 2007).

Thus I will argue that at the particular historical moment in which I was examining Barbadian public culture (2002–8), the homosexual regularly operated as a seminal figure through which a complex array of local, national, and transnational social, political, and economic tensions were aligned, related, and defined (or redefined). Specifically, I argue that it is no coincidence that homosexuality was increasingly debated in public contexts at this historical juncture because Barbados faced major social and economic challenges in its marginal position relative to other international political and economic alliances such as the North American Free Trade Agreement (NAFTA) and the European Union (EU). Barbados was also facing regional challenges through its participation in the CARICOM Single Market and Economy (CSME), which is similar to the EU in its objectives to create stronger, more globally competitive economies but among participating Caribbean nations. These realignments (or potential realignments) of political and economic power were bringing about significant changes in the socio-economic fabric of life of many Bajans, resulting in what some observers claimed was a submissive, subordinated, or 'feminized' (defined through a heteropatriarchal lens) economy. Like many other societies, Barbados was also undergoing rapid technological changes through the increasing presence of computer, television, and mobile communication technologies, which in turn linked Barbadians to multiple, globally circulating ideas, values, and identities relating to sexuality. Yet such changes and challenges were not necessarily all that new for Barbados and the rest of the Caribbean because these societies have been forged through the transnational commerce of colonialism, forced and voluntary migration of different ethnic and racialized groups, and exposure to multiple and often competing moral value systems for over five hundred years. Questions about what is 'natural' or 'unnatural' sex have been present in these societies and their attendant discourses of respectable citizenship since their colonial inception, but in recent years a particular incarnation of the 'homosexual' has become the most visible index of (dis)respectability, (im)morality, and social (in)stability in particular media and public discourses. This silent, spectral, yet ever-present entity has become the new 'pariah' amongst some individuals and groups who are unhappy with the current socio-economic situation and produce a nationalist nostalgia for return to a mythic past of a communal, heterosexual, and homogenous Christian society.

In locating the homosexual as a key trope or metaphor through which an array of social economic and political tensions and changes are organized, I hope to open up the scope of dialogue on sexuality in the Caribbean. Although sexual diversity is thankfully no longer a marginal topic in Caribbean social studies (see Glave 2008, Kempadoo 2004, Lewis 2003b, and Sharpe and Pinto 2006 for recent excellent overviews and/or collections of research on this topic), research in the social sciences that goes beyond the heterosexual norm has, for the most part, focused on either marginalization of and/or violence towards sexual minorities like gays or lesbians (usually explained in relation to historical contexts of slavery, conservative religious beliefs, and/or deeply heteronormative definitions of gender identities), or on local ethno-racial sexual identifications and practices that do not align neatly with Euro-American models of gender and sexuality (that is, Gloria Wekker's important research [2006] on *mati* relationships among working-class women in Suriname). While these are important and valuable contributions that give voice to what was practically invisible in social science research on the Caribbean twenty years' ago, there is still little research that explores in detail how sexual desires, identities, and prejudices are produced, organized, and related through multiple sites in a specific society, how these sites are both local and transnational in their assemblages, and how they assemble, perform, and create or recreate particular formations of the homosexual that, when reiterated and re-performed in relation to other local and global sexual formations, re-inscribe, realign, and/or disrupt these formations, producing new formative possibilities.[8]

One notable feature of most Bajan public debates on homosexuality, whether they occurred in the pages of the daily newspaper the *Nation*, or in a townhall meeting discussing the decriminalization of homosexuality, was that the homosexual was almost always an invisible figure, a ghostly haunting without flesh and bones, and, most important, without voice. With the important exception of a few self-described 'out, loud, and proud queens' (*queen* is a local term with multiple contextual meanings but, broadly put, refers to effeminate gay men, some of whom dress and perform regularly as women; for more on this, see chapter 5), the pages, airwaves, and stages of Barbados were bereft of voices that identified themselves as gay, lesbian, or homosexual. Yet the reasons for this apparent absence may not be as straightforward as one might assume (that is, simply due to widespread homophobia). First, we may need to parse the term *public* into different realms or spaces; in other words, we need to acknowledge different forms of public space constituted through the privileging of particular discourses, identifications, and/or performances. For example, public spaces constituted through the printed text of mainstream daily newspapers or town-hall meetings organized by government health and welfare agencies may privilege particular subject formations of respectability and status (with their attendant heteronormative privileges), whereas other public spaces such as the street or rum shop in a working-class neighbourhood may (or may not) support different subject formations of respectability and status. Thus, what or who may appear to be silenced in the arena of one public space should not be assumed to be indicative of nationwide silence or some shared national moral code.

We may also need to rethink the parameters of the claim itself: When asserting that homosexuals, gays, and lesbians are invisible or silent in particular public contexts, we must be attentive to the dangers of sexual terminologies and *their* silent but powerful histories, movements, and attachments. In other words, if I observe that there are no gay or lesbian voices in (certain) Bajan public debates, what do I mean by *gay* and *lesbian*? Do these terms carry within them a Euro-American configuration that is produced through a particular arrangement of gendered, sexed, raced, and classed relations? Do *gay* and *lesbian* convey different meanings in a post-colonial society like Barbados than in an urban North American context? How and where do the more publicly visible Bajan queens fit into local sex or gender alignments?

With these questions in mind, the second half of this book (chapters 4 to 7) focuses on the 'invisible' lives of self-identified gay men and the more publicly visible Bajan queens. In examining the advice of a local gay-identified bed-and-breakfast owner on gay life in Barbados, the drama of some queens' cellphone romances with Jamaican men, and the life stories of a range of queens and gay Bajan men, I flesh out another central theme of this book: While sexual diversity in Barbados is immersed in, is partially productive of, and is produced through contemporary Euro-American gendered and sexual politics and identities (which are produced and circulated through mobile bodies of tourists, workers, lovers, relatives, communications technologies, and liberal democratic political and economic policies), this diversity is simultaneously produced through and in relation to local and regional gendered and sexual-identity politics. Such politics require us to acknowledge the ongoing influence of a colonized past and its attendant gendered, classed, raced, and cultural dynamics that produce unstable, unpredictable, multiple possibilities of sexual subjectivities. I argue that the Bajan 'sexscape' (to coin a term from Appadurai [1996]) is neither an illustration of a creolized or hybrid culture nor a reflection of a pluralistic compendium of multiple, discrete cultures since both of these theoretical approaches risk oversimplification, as noted by Slocum and Thomas in their excellent historical review of Caribbean anthropology (2003). These approaches tend either to emphasize separate, unintegrated cultural communities existing alongside each other (pluralism), implying an incompatible and dysfunctional sociocultural system, or to emphasize the way in which Caribbean societies have produced a singular culture that seamlessly blends together the influences of their diverse ethnic and racial backgrounds (creolization), thus often obscuring ongoing significant cultural, class, and racial hierarchies (Slocum and Thomas 2003). Rather, I suggest that the relative visibility of queens, and invisibility of gays and lesbians, in certain public contexts and the different opinions on what daily life is like for queer people in Barbados are the result of an ongoing tension between differentially located and produced subjectivities and values that are pieced together in myriad, contextually shifting ways by individuals who are marginalized by virtue of their non-heteronormative desires and the particular limitations placed on these desires and produced through neocolonial economic, racial, sexual, and gendered structures of inequality.

My arguments are deeply influenced by transnational feminist analysis such as M. Jacqui Alexander's writing on Caribbean sexual politics and more generally by the productive debates that have arisen through the lively intersections of queer and globalization studies. One of the major critiques of earlier incarnations of queer theory focused on its tendency to erase or overlook significant material and economic inequalities under the universalizing rubric of *queer*. Jose Quiroga's trenchant argument (2000) against the universality of gay/lesbian or queer subjects and politics and his reconceptualization of sexual subject formation through the geopolitical relations of global capital and the nation state provides an excellent counterbalance to writings of some gay and lesbian studies scholars who, often unwittingly, reproduce a Eurocentric perspective as they analyse the rise of gay and lesbian communities and activism in non-Western places.[9] My analytical framework is also influenced by recent investigations of sexual minority activism and movements in post-colonial societies like South Africa (Hoad 2007), Nicaragua (Howe 2002), Bolivia (Wright 2000), and Martinique (Jones 2009), which do a good job of identifying and analysing the complex, productive, and problematic ways in which local activists, groups, and individuals strategically adapt, interpret, and are constrained through their interventions with international LGBT, human rights, and development agencies whose language of progress, liberation, and freedom often presupposes particular kinds of sexual subjects (and their attendant rights) that are constituted through particular political and economic frameworks.

While my objective is to complicate these sexual, gendered, and racialized binaries of the First World versus those of the Third World, I am also cognizant of my own position as a white, male, gay-identified researcher located in a

North American university, writing about sexuality and gender in a post-colonial nation state that is situated (albeit problematically) in the global South. While I am trying to write against the transnational transfer of hegemonic discourses about sexual identities, differences, and alliances produced within metropolitan countries, I am simultaneously embedded within them, thus placed in a position with particular privileges and limitations that are produced in and through my relationship to colonial and imperial formations and their debris (Stoler 2008). I write out of a desire to challenge and change assumptions about sexual identities, desires, and alliances in transnational contexts, but I acknowledge that my own gendered, racialized, and sexual positioning may well indeed blind me to different components of experience and thus perpetuate certain silences and erasures as I attempt to write across borders. One of the silences of which I am particularly aware in the following chapters pertains to women and female same-sex relationships and orientations. As I note in chapter 1, most of the public debates that I observed in Barbados addressed male homosexuality. However, to suggest that the visibility accorded to male homosexuality is indicative of an absence of lesbianism from the public imagination is to fail to theorize this absence from the location of the feminist enquiry that might consider the social conditions that enable the appearance of such an absence. This crucial question and the topic of female same-sex relations and identifications remains underdeveloped in this book owing to my engagement with a homosocial world of mostly men and queens, which may reflect in part the organization of local sex-gender orders and in part my own ethnocentric gendered and sexual motivations and assumptions about whom to seek out and talk to in order to answer my questions.

The Outline of the Chapters

This book begins by documenting and analysing some of the public debates over the rights versus the threat of homosexuals in Barbados. In chapter 1, I focus on Bajan 'feedback' media (phone-in shows, and opinion columnists and letters to the editor in the daily newspapers), in which a great deal of talk about homosexuals was taking place in the early years of the new millennium owing to a combination of local and international events. One of the interesting themes that emerges in this chapter is the way in which these mostly negative media representations of the homosexual are connected to discussions of perceived social and economic changes occurring in Barbados, such that the homosexual becomes the bogeyman of post-millennial angst over rampant consumerism, national self-determination, and neoliberal discourses of globalization. Chapter 2 shifts to another public arena, a series of public meetings organized by the

National HIV/AIDS Commission to discuss removing Barbados's criminal laws against homosexuality in order to reduce the stigma of homosexuality, which would hopefully result in better prevention and control of the spread of HIV/AIDS. I argue that, in spite of the attempt by some medical and governmental officials to support the rights of homosexuals, at these public meetings and in the media reports on them the HIV prevention framework through which these rights were advocated inadvertently re-inscribed the connection between homosexuality and HIV and reinforced a popular image of the homosexual as diseased and dangerous. Chapter 3 focuses more closely on the discourse of sexual rights that emerged in decriminalization discussions and examines how rights were interpreted in different ways by differently positioned groups in Barbados. I argue that we cannot assume that sexual rights have a universal value, and, in fact, in post-colonial societies like Barbados certain rights discourses can be interpreted as hostile and/or connected to the political interests of former colonizing powers. I then explore a method that may be used to circumvent this type of critique, in which the principles of international rights discourses may be remade in the vernacular, that is, by finding ways in which new ideas may be framed and presented in terms of existing cultural norms, values, and practices (Merry 2006b).

The second half of this book (chapters 4 to 7) focuses on non-heteronormative lives in Barbados. Too often, in much of the work on queer globalization and sexual rights, there is a paucity of research on the lived effects of the negative public representations of the homosexual, or we find terms such as *gay* and *lesbian* applied uncritically in local contexts. Thus, while the first half of this book focuses on examining the circulation of the homosexual in public debates about society, state, and social change, the second half of this book focuses on the lived effects of these public discourses on those who are labelled *homosexual* or *gay*. Through interviews, anecdotes, and stories by and about differentially positioned, self-identified queens and gays in Barbados, I begin to show some of the complexity of the lives that are constituted through these dense local, regional, and global flows, inequalities, and interchanges. In chapters that focus on a Bajan bed-and-breakfast owner's advice to tourists on how to deal with local men (chapter 4), on the publicly visible past and present daily life of Bajan queens compared to the invisible life of gay men (chapter 5), on the drama of the romantic relationships between Jamaican men and Bajan queens in which cellphones play an important role in both initiating and ending them (chapter 6), and on the life stories of three self-identified gay men (chapter 7) what emerges is not a singular, identical definition of or position on sexuality, desire, and gender and their organization and operations in daily Bajan life. Rather, across these chapters we find similar intersections of local, regional, and globally circulating sexual identities, the centrality of the theme of respectability in Barbadian daily life, and its complex relationship to performances of masculinity and femininity that are embedded in racialized, classed, and heteronormative structures of inequality. In the conclusion I review the main arguments of this book and focus on the unstable and complex operations of respectability in the post-colonial nation state and its uneven effects on those who are rendered marginal or invisible through its heteropatriarchal norms.

Chapter 1

The Spectral Homosexual in Barbadian Feedback Media

During a series of research trips to Barbados between 2002 and 2005, I was struck by the saturation of media coverage on homosexuality. Homosexuality was being discussed in a variety of Barbadian media sites ranging from newspapers to the Internet and radio. During my longest visit, from September 2004 to April 2005, I cut out and filed every news item from the *Nation* (one of Barbados's two daily newspapers) that included the words *homosexual* or *gay*. By the end of that seven-month period my file folder had 355 clippings, which amounted to approximately 1.5 news items per issue. In retrospect, perhaps I should not have been so surprised: gays and lesbians were hot news topics in many media outlets around the world at this time. Much of the news in the *Nation*, on the radio, and in Internet sites such as JustBajan.com focused on the same-sex rights and justice struggles occurring elsewhere around the globe, such as the same-sex marriage debates in Europe, Canada, and the United States, various Christian denominations' battles over the ordainment of gay or lesbian priests and ministers, and the ongoing battle against HIV/AIDS. What I found interesting was the way in which these overseas affairs were localized through letters to the editor, editorials, op-ed columns, and online bulletin boards where opinions were expressed about these events and their potential effects on Barbadian society. However, homosexuality was also part of local news events. During 2004–5, three public forums were held by the National HIV/AIDS Commission of Barbados to elicit feedback on Professor Mickey Walrond's 'Report on the Legal, Ethical, and Socio-economic Issues Relevant to HIV/AIDS in Barbados' (2004). The report, which was commissioned by the Attorney General's office, made numerous suggestions to address the issues, and among them was support for the decriminalization of homosexuality[1] in order to reduce the stigma and fear associated with the virus. These forums generated a great deal of coverage in the op-ed and letters-to-the-editor sections of the *Nation* (these forums will be discussed in greater detail in chapter 3).

Much, but by no means all, of this feedback or opinion media, whether internationally or locally focused, valued homosexuality negatively: *wrong*, *immoral*, *dangerous*, *corrupt*, *perverted*, and *sin* were some of the more common terms used to describe same-sex identities and practices. Furthermore, in all this media talk no voice of a homosexual from Barbados was to be found. No letters to the editor, online bulletin board postings, or op-ed columns were signed by anyone who said that he or she was gay, homosexual or lesbian.[2] Furthermore, there were no organized associations or groups dedicated primarily to supporting gay and lesbian rights in Barbados to which reporters and/or editors could turn for a response.[3]

In this chapter I focus primarily on these feedback and opinion sections of Barbadian newspapers, radio shows, and online news sites. Through critical discourse analysis of this material I think we can gain some insight into why homosexuality appears to be a problem in contemporary Barbados. This will allow us to see beyond just the negative positioning of homosexuality – the anti-gay rhetoric – and gain insight into these representational frameworks through which homosexuality comes to be signified. However, I will also try to show that it is important to locate these representational frameworks in relation to knowledge of Barbados's colonial history and its current, somewhat marginal position in a larger global ecumenism celebrating neoliberal democracy and free enterprise capitalism. In particular, I am interested in the gendered and sexual effects of current socio-political, cultural, and economic configurations in Barbados as they are located within larger historical and global flows. I will argue that hegemonic discourses about homosexuality in Barbadian media are produced through a heterosexual patriarchal logic originating in a first-wave form of globalization known as colonialism, but which has been reproduced *and challenged* through the turbulent, uneven processes of economic, political, and cultural globalization over the past twenty years.

These discourses, combined with the absence of local gay or lesbian voices in the media, result in what I call a spectral sexuality that haunts the Barbadian mediascapes, where a threatening, perverted, and/or sick sexualized body or group of bodies are continually incarnated in discourse but never fully instantiated in the flesh. These deviant ghostly bodies haunt the dominant discourse of a national body that is imagined to be heterosexual and masculine and perceived to be under attack from outside and inside forces (cf. Mosse 1985; Alexander 1994, 1997). This haunting is produced by global political, economic, and social forces that are contributing towards a greater socio-economic chasm between a small elite business class, a stressed and fragile middle class, and a growing class of working poor and/or unemployed in Barbados and around the world (cf. Kimmel 2003) . These perceptions and experiences of destabilization increase the surveillance of and concern about who is and what is the source of this socio-economic instability. For a variety of historically contextual reasons, homosexuals have come to be, for some Barbadians, the bogeymen of a turbulent and stressful modernity in the new millennium, absorbing and representing all that is wrong with contemporary social life in a developing nation that is located on the margins of Euro-American nation states' economic and political programs.

It is important to note that in this chapter I am focusing only on the ways in which homosexuality is discussed in a particular media genre (opinion or feedback media). This material should not be interpreted as indicative of the way in which homosexuality is viewed by all Barbadians, nor is it reflective of a cultural belief system about sexuality or homosexuality. Media discourses, as noted by numerous media studies analysts, are particular sites in which information is structured by and through local, national, and global social, political, and economic forces (Hall 1997; Henry and Tator 2002; Macdonald 2003; Van Dijk 1988). As Debra Spitulnik (1997) has noted, exploring the social circulation of media discourse outside the contexts of direct media consumption can reveal diverse, creative reworkings of media discourses. In other words, while it is important to understand how and why certain discourses are privileged – the goal of this chapter being to understand the 'logic' of privileged homophobic discourses – we must not forget that there are multiple subjective lenses through which these discourses may be interpreted, resisted, and/or transformed. Some of the different interpretations of these hegemonic discourses will be explored in greater detail in chapters 4, 5, and 6.

I begin by exploring some of this media talk in more detail, providing three examples that highlight some of the key frames through which homosexuality is negatively articulated. Following this, I will analyse some common themes of these texts in relation to the gendered and sexualized contours of local and global social, economic, and political dynamics.

The System Is Saying, 'Let Everything Go ...'

The first example of negative articulation of homosexuality is drawn from a news, current affairs, and entertainment website for Barbadians, www.justbajan.com, which carries a discussion forum where the web server posts questions and people are invited to respond. A large number of comments (over 1,300 in May 2004) were posted in reaction to the question, 'Should gay people be allowed to get married?' The majority of comments were not supportive and in many cases included critical statements about homosexuality generally. One posting seemed a bit out of place but generated some interesting responses: an individual named 'Lost Boy,' who identified himself as an American male, said that he was planning to visit Barbados and wanted to know if gay tourists were welcomed there (leading me to assume that he was not a Barbadian citizen). He received numerous responses. One reply came from Mr X, twenty-five years of age, who identified himself as a Barbadian male from Oistins (a town in the south of the island): 'Would you welcome someone in your own country whose behaviour you consider to be immoral? ... Would you welcome the Taliban to your home, and if not, why not? I hope you get the point. Gay people are not welcome by the majority of Bajans.' Another response came from 'Assassin,' who identified himself as a Barbadian male from Bridgetown (the capital city of Barbados):

> People like you might think our law against homosexuals is wrong, but if you respect our laws and by extension the people of this country, you will abide by the laws of this country. You seem to be of the opinion that the 'poor, pitiful, uneducated' people of Barbados should be down on our hands and knees kissing the ground tourists like yourselves walk on, just because you are willing to come and spend money in our country ... Keep that pro-homosexual propaganda drivel in your own country; we don't condone it here. Why should anyone listen to what America has to say about other countries' laws? Have you ever really sat down and analysed the moral morass that your country currently exists in? Do you really believe that a sovereign nation should take hints and legal advice from a country like that?

The second example of negative articulation comes from a Caribbean Broadcasting Corporation (CBC) radio talk show that took place in November 2004. The topic of the program was, 'Has Barbados become an immoral society?' on which the host elaborated by stating, 'Are we too tolerant of homosexuality, prostitution, and other so-called perverted trends now evident in Barbados?' The vast majority of the callers to the show agreed that Barbados was indeed becoming immoral and that immorality could be defined primarily in terms of homosexuality and prostitution. During the program some callers provided explanations of why this type of 'immorality' was taking over Barbados: One caller stated that 'there is a global agenda to legalize everything which was taboo before. This is something that is being pushed a lot in the state, to make everything that we consider wrong right ... In other words, the system is saying, "Let everything go. Whatever you wanna do, do." My position on prostitution and homosexuality is that God does not approve of it ...' Another caller identified a different reason for these problems: 'At the core we've become selfish ... it's a direction we've been going in progressively ... There's the consumerism that is driving most of the issues relating to the economy...; it's leading us down the path to perversion.' A third caller made a similar comment: '[Men and women are] involved in all this kinky sex because it's a reflection of where we are in this society… It's this consumerism. People have big houses, nuff [a lot of] money, they're bored, don't know what to do with themselves, so this is what they do.'

The third example is drawn from one of the flurry of letters sent to the editor of the *Nation* between December 2004 and March 2005, responding to the recommendation to decriminalize homosexuality and prostitution in the just published Walrond report. Alicia Smith[4] began her letter this way: 'It was the former United States Surgeon General, Dr Benjamin [*sic*] Koop, who cautioned that the anal canal is not intended for use as a sexual orifice, given its very thin and fragile lining. This together with the disease profile and early death of homosexuals through hepatitis, liver disease, gastro-intestinal parasites, sexually transmitted diseases … [the list goes on] should be of particular concern to Professor Walrond, who should oppose homosexuality on purely medical grounds … We must not forsake our enduring Christian morality for the bigotry of secularism … It will be tyrannical of the government to support [this recommendation]' (*The Nation*, 12 January 2005).

Themes of Feedback Media

The above examples of comments and letters convey at least five oft repeated and related themes about homosexuality found in Barbadian feedback media during the period. First, many refer to Barbadian law as 'proof' of the illegitimacy of homosexuality.[5] Second, the laws are claimed to be representative of the nation's Christian morality,[6] thus implying more or less overtly a religious national culture and linking homosexuality to the moral and cultural health of the nation. The third theme is often found in relation to the second; it compares the moral health of Barbados to other nations and often finds the latter to be inferior, such as Assassin's reference to the United States as being in a 'moral morass' due primarily to its 'pro-homosexual' stance (which, of course, is an interesting interpretation of American public discourses on homosexuality, given President Bush's statements at that time on heterosexual marriage as the bedrock of civilization). Sometimes the nation of Barbados is positioned against a less specified, more global consortium of powerful nations or interests, as demonstrated in the comments of the CBC radio-program caller who identified the 'global agenda to legalize everything which was taboo before.' In either case, the nation of Barbados is compared to politically and economically powerful, but morally corrupt, nations.

In contrast to the third theme, the fourth theme locates sources of immoral behaviours like homosexuality *within* Barbados. However, these sources are, at the same time, recognized as having been produced, affected, or impacted by global influences. For example, we hear the radio-show callers who note the rise of 'rampant consumerism' as the generator of 'bad' behaviours such as selfishness, boredom, and listlessness, which then lead to 'kinky sex' practices like homosexuality and visits to prostitutes. Finally, many of these commentaries explicitly describe the homosexual body as a 'diseased' body – through references to HIV/AIDS, other health problems like alcoholism, and/or 'unclean' sexual practices like anal sex – and then claim that this is therefore a lifestyle or behaviour that is unhealthy and therefore dangerous to Barbadian society.

In order to understand how and why these themes are popular in feedback media, we need to identify a series of changes that have occurred in Barbados over the past twenty to twenty-five years, related to historical and contemporary global economic and social transformations. The first of these transformations is political-economic. Jacqui Alexander's groundbreaking work on the socio-sexual and political effects of tourism on Bahamian and Trinidadian nationalist discourses provides a key foundation for thinking about the way in which Barbadian media discourses about homosexuality have emerged. Alexander demonstrates that homosexuality has been a central factor in structuring nationalist discourses of identity through modes of criminal 'spectacularization' and/or erasure as governments try to lure transnational capital investments (1994, 1997). I argue that a similar situation exists in Barbados where the effects of internationally influenced local political and economic strategies are reshaping gendered and sexual relations, such that the male homosexual[7] is quickly becoming the internal 'other' for certain sectors of the Barbadian population; he has become a the figure who threatens the legitimacy and order of the Barbadian nation state, the one who represents all that is imposed, colonial, and unjustly empowered in a society undergoing rapid socio-economic change. In line with Patton's (1997) and Yingling's (1997) powerful analyses of the way in which early discourses around HIV/AIDS contributed to moral panics, reinforcing heteronormative, racially exclusive, and deeply classed nationalisms, I am arguing that Barbadian feedback media discourses about the homosexual are indicative of a moral panic among some Barbadians that is being produced in relation to rapid internal and external social, political, and economic transformations, which reinforce for some, but not all, a long-standing perception of marginality and powerlessness in their own society and abroad. This marginality may be perceived in terms of race, gender, and political and/or economic status and reflects a colonial legacy of racial, economic, and political subordination. A sense of increasing marginalization within a nation that is locally and internationally touted as a Caribbean success story in terms of its wealth, political stability, and social infrastructure (as stated repeatedly by the prime minister at that time and found in popular international reports such as U.S. Department of State Country Profiles)[8] may lead certain sectors of the population to scapegoat or stigmatize particular groups whose different ideas and/or practices can be blamed for contributing to what is wrong with their world. For these sectors, moral decay is linked to the 'feminization' of the economy and public life, domains that are perceived to be traditionally heterosexual and masculine.

This line of thinking requires further enquiry into economic and political changes and the symbolic framing of those changes as they are occurring in Barbados. Carla Freeman, in her account of women working in the rapidly growing employment sector of informatics (data entry and call service centres) in Barbados, notes that Caribbean countries like Barbados have been marginalized by transnational economic treaties like the North American Free Trade Agreement and the European Union, resulting in ever-increasing dependency on a service-based economy where informatics and tourism are two of the leading employment sectors (Freeman 2000, 23 and 31). These arenas employ growing numbers of women in low-wage jobs and are thus often classified as 'feminized' economic sectors (Freeman 2000, 44).

Furthermore, Freeman notes that popular discourses (as well as more esoteric theories) of globalization are couched in masculinist, heteronormative frames; for example, we hear talk of the importance of 'penetrating virgin markets.' These are narratives in which power operates in masculinized acts of non-reciprocal penetration. Expressions of globalization valorize the norms of global finance, telecommunications, production, and trade that are associated with Western capitalist masculinity. In much of the globalization discourses 'the local' is a developing country that has no choice but to 'submit' to the power of the developed nations and the inevitable 'righteous' force of capitalism and its attendant social policies. In other words, high-level global restructuring is constructed as a masculinized domain that is characterized by high-tech mobility, autonomy, and challenging opportunities, but local labour forces situated mostly in developing nation states are feminized through their servitude, powerlessness, and lack of personal space and autonomy (Freeman 2001, 1014–16; see also Kimmel 2003, 604). In nation states with a history of colonization these are gendered and racialized tropes of powerlessness that resonate with a not too distant past, but the old transparent discourse of the colonizing civilizations' 'natural' superiority (rendering them easily identifiable as the villain) has been replaced by the more opaque liberal rhetoric of free markets, individual freedom, and equal opportunity, rhetoric that is endorsed by the government of Barbados;[9] this makes it more difficult to explain why it is so hard to make ends meet or who is to blame.

Thus I am suggesting that due to an economy which is perceived to be increasingly more 'feminine,' exploitative, and/or subservient as it shifts towards service-industry-based labour, some Barbadians feel that there are fewer and fewer 'appropriate' (masculine) employment opportunities available to them. The shift to a service sector economy not only creates the perception of a more feminized economy but also feminizes national identity (in a patriarchal interpretation whereby *feminized* is associated with a subordinated, 'please the master' status).[10] A nation state that accepts homosexuality is, from this perspective, proof of a powerless, penetrated, emasculated loser on the world stage. This is what I sense in some of the anti-homosexual comments like those of Assassin when, for example, he asks if Americans like Lost Boy assume that Bajans are submissive because they rely on tourism, and will accept homosexuals just because it is okay to do so in the United States, or that Bajans are so desperate for U.S. dollars that they will accept any and everything.

When Assassin tells Lost Boy to 'keep that pro-homosexual propaganda drivel in your own country … Do you really believe that a sovereign nation should take hints and legal advice from a country like that?' or when the caller on the CBC radio program discusses how 'there is a global agenda to legalize everything which was taboo before,' there lies both recognition and critique of a post-colonial society's place in the contemporary global ecumene. These Barbadians are aware of gay and lesbian activism around the world (as mentioned above, local newspapers often contain reports of controversies and debates occurring elsewhere in the world), but the reports are localized, that is, rendered meaningful in relation to local socio-sexual issues through particular moral frameworks. The overseas LGBT activism is often referred to as part of a 'gay rights' agenda, or a pro-gay 'system' that is supported by (or controls) the political leaders of Euro-American nations who are very powerful and are trying to impose their economic, political, and moral (or immoral) interests on the government and people of Barbados.

This perspective should not be summarily dismissed as a conspiratorial fantasy. Pressure to reform the laws against homosexuality in numerous Caribbean nation states is coming from organizations like Amnesty International, Human Rights Watch, and the International Lesbian and Gay Association who critique national governments according to human rights principles and agreements developed through supranational bodies like the United Nations. However, as Matthew Engelke has observed, international human rights activism can have mixed results. Engelke (1999) notes that discourses of human rights are wound up in complex political and cultural dynamics that are simultaneously local and transnational and often carry within them the accumulated effects of colonial relations that have been perpetuated through the unequal economic and social outcomes of recent forms of globalization. Engelke suggests that one of the reasons President Robert Mugabe of Zimbabwe was so persistent in identifying homosexuality as 'un-African' and not defensible as a right was so that his party could claim to be the only moral authority able to rescue a society 'under threat' from an easily recognized outside foe, the political, social, and economic legacies of colonialism. Developed nations are once again utilizing their political and economic force to bully a developing nation into adopting their social and political agendas. Assassin's comments and those of other Barbadian feedback-media contributors indicate a similar perception of and rhetorical resistance to forced submission to Western political, economic, and moral agendas that emasculate and thus humiliate their nation's status. I will return to discuss the complex production and interpretation of sexual rights discourses in more detail in chapter 3.

However, a feminized, submissive national economy or identity that is forcibly imposed by an external power (which reproduces tropes of colonial relations of power) is not the only way in which the homosexual comes to stand for the social decay of the nation. A different, albeit related, connection between morality, homosexuality, and the national economy appears via the 'problem' of vulgar materialism in contemporary Barbados, as, for example, when the radio-show caller stated that 'consumerism … is driving most of the issues relating to the economy … it's leading us down the path to perversion.' These commentaries are critical of a particular material practice (consumption) resulting from the government-induced shift to a free-market, individualist, and privatized economy. In these comments, uncontrolled consumption is creating a more selfish, decadent, and amoral society. The commentaries are different from those presented in the previous paragraph in two ways: (1) The homosexual threat comes from or is produced *within* Barbados rather than existing externally, and thus there is tacit acknowledgment of homosexuality as an already existing phenomenon in Barbadian society; and (2) they employ a form of nationalist nostalgia, in which a 'proper,' heterosexual, family-oriented, Christian, and communal Barbadian nation of the past is compared to an 'immoral,' consumer-driven, privatized, secular, and pan-sexual Barbados of the present. Socio-economic change is evaluated via a kind of sexual barometer where the possibility of accepting (homo)sexual practices by the minders of the nation state indicates a precipitous fall from an imagined national past of heterosexual, familial unity. Scholars of nationalism elsewhere have noted the importance of nationalist nostalgia myths not in terms of their authenticity or inauthenticity but rather in the ways in which they are related to perceptions of racial, economic, and/or political empowerment or disempowerment by those who circulate them (Hage 2000; Mackey 2002; Povinelli 2002). The ending of these nostalgic nationalist narratives is usually the same – the moral decay of the nation – although there are different indexes or measurements of that decay. According to some of the Bajan feedback-media commentators, the clearest sign is sexual perversion, which ranges from 'kinky sex acts' to the state's legitimization of homosexuality.

Notably, these commentaries focus almost exclusively on male homosexuality; I found very few references to lesbianism in feedback media. This is not surprising. As numerous scholars have noted, since most nationalisms are constructed through heterosexual, fraternal, and patriarchal frameworks, men who want to have sex with men are construed as the greatest internal threat to the reproductive fantasies of the nationalist imaginary (Mosse 1985; Parker et al. 1992; Yuval-Davis 1997). From this perspective, women are supposed to occupy the private, domestic familial spaces of the national imaginary, and their sexuality is only imagined as heterosexually reproductive, submissive, and receptive to their husband's needs and desires. While female homosexuality is seen by nationalists as a corruption of femininity, it is nevertheless powerless and non-threatening to men and less of a challenge to heteropatriarchy than is male homosexuality (Kempadoo 2004, 47). Or, to put it in the context of Ms Smith's letter, lesbians appear to be no threat to the fragile male anus.[11]

These online commentaries, phone calls, and letters to the editor thus contribute to a hegemonic discourse in which the internal or external male homosexual serves a particular semiotic strategy, acting as the key indicator of downward movement of the social respectability of the nation. Yet this is a 'spectral' homosexual, a depersonalized, unnamed entity who is observed to be demanding and gaining rights in powerful, wealthy, but morally corrupt, Euro-American nations and whose existence is now acknowledged in Barbadian public contexts – but only in one particular incarnation as a feminized male body that infects the legitimate hetero-masculine national body of Barbados, indexing the fall from a 'phantasmatic,' past, national unity (Ivy 1995). These spectral sexual deviants are critical components of nationalist imaginaries. As Marilyn Ivy notes in her analysis of Japanese nationalism, the nation can never be fully realized; it is a 'phantasmatic' structure itself that produces, indeed requires, inscriptions of its own marginality in its narratives of cultural unity and homogeneity. The figure of the ghost 'spectrally embodies … the recalcitrance of representation itself, the impossibility of stabilizing meaning … Ghosts are haunting precisely because they reveal an inability to control representation' (1995, 165). In Barbadian media discourses we often find the homosexual haunting the words of some Barbadians who desire an ideal of national cultural and economic solidarity, yet simultaneously reveal their own social, economic, and political marginality through their identification of the villains, the sexualized bogeymen, who ostensibly control 'the system.' Their own sense of disempowerment, however real or imagined, is produced through the prism of a nationalist political-economic myth that promises prosperity and equality for all citizens who embrace the values of free market capitalism, and blames the individual who does not prosper in such a climate.

That this spectral homosexual is occupying mainstream media discourses at this particular point in time is due not only to the unpredictable effects of a global hegemonic heterosexualized masculinity in local contexts (Kimmel 2003) but also to its presence in other gendered and sexed discourses circulating through global and local media coverage over the past fifteen to twenty years. As noted above, these include increased reporting on international gay and lesbian activism in many nation states to which Barbadians have emigrated (and whose nationals have moved to Barbados) and the ongoing presence of HIV/AIDS, still identified as a 'gay' disease in parts of Barbados (more on this in the next chapter).

Another notable gendered and sexed discourse that influences opinions on homosexuality is Christianity. The regular presence of the Bible, God, and Christian values in Barbadian feedback-media discussions of homosexuality indicates the significant presence of religious values in public discourses that assess acceptable gendered and sexual behaviour. According to the Barbados Population and Housing Census of 2000, the majority of Barbadians identify themselves as belonging to a Christian denomination[12] (Barbados Statistical Service 2000, 34). I was told by a number of my interviewees that until recently the majority of Christian Barbadians were Anglican, but American-based Pentecostal charismatic Christian groups were increasing in popularity[13] (see also Robbins 2004). As Sullivan-Bloom points out in her research on homophobia in American Christianity, evangelical and fundamentalist Christians have focused energetically on organizing and communicating their position on the sin of homosexuality and gay marriage and are increasingly sophisticated in their political influence, knowledge of media formats, and control of media technologies (2009).

There are numerous additional circuits of popular talk about gender and (homo)sexuality beyond the scope of this chapter, such as the lyrics of popular music styles like dance hall, calypso, and hip hop, which interact with, reflect, and/or influence feedback-media opinions (see Gutzmore 2004 and Lafont 2009). Once again, it is important to keep in mind that these various discourses on sex and gender in the media are always unstable and always intersecting with other kinds of social, political, and economic talk, rendering the positioning of gendered and sexed identities unstable themselves. However, in the early years of the new millennium it was clear that differentially located and temporally generated discourses circulating through Barbadian feedback media had coalesced to produce a similar moral positioning on homosexuality, with the cumulative effect of further marginalizing it from the position of respectable citizenship.

Conclusion

As Henry and Tator note, 'we cannot ignore the media's crucial role in influencing and reinforcing attitudes and opinions' (2002, 7). In this chapter I have tried to examine the reasons for a relatively consistent positioning of the homosexual as a threat to Barbadian society in feedback media at a particular historical moment.[14] I argued that Barbados was facing a turbulent moment in its history through economic challenges with regard to its marginal position relative to other political-economic alliances such as the North American Free Trade Agreement and the European Union; it was also facing regional challenges through its participation in the CARICOM Single Market and Economy, all of which were bringing about significant changes in the socio-economic fabric of life and producing, for some, a submissive, subordinated, or feminized economy (defined through a heteropatriarchal lens). Like many other small societies, Barbados was also undergoing rapid technological changes through the increasing presence of computer, television, and mobile communication technologies, which in turn linked Barbadians to multiple globally circulating ideas, values, and identities relating to sexuality. Yet these changes and challenges were not necessarily all that new for Barbados, because this is a society that has been forged through the transnational commerce of colonialism, the migration of different ethno-racial groups, and exposure to multiple and often competing value systems for over five hundred years. Questions about what is natural or unnatural sex have been present in societies like Barbados from their colonial inception, but in recent years a particular incarnation of the homosexual has become the most visible index of immorality and social instability in particular media discourses. This silent, spectral, yet ever-present entity has become the new pariah among individuals and groups who are unhappy with the current socio-economic situation and strive to return to a mythic past of a communal, heterosexual, and homogenous Christian nation.

Although these opinions dominated feedback media, there were notable exceptions that challenged anti-gay sentiment, which were written by laypersons. Assuming a uniform societal or national position on homosexuality,

based on patterns of discourse in a particular media genre, is deeply problematic; subsequent chapters will hopefully demonstrate the complex ways in
which sexuality is positioned in relation to gender in everyday talk amongst
individuals, networks, and diverse communities in Barbados, which therefore
acknowledges the possibility of multiple, contextually generated moral frameworks operating throughout these different communities and networks.

Chapter 2

Gender, Sexuality, and HIV/AIDS Discourses in Barbados

In this chapter I engage with the local-national-transnational dynamic of gendered and sexual identity formations and practices through an exploration of the way in which the Barbadian state has become involved in the sexuality of its citizens (an involvement that is also and always gendered) through activities and statements related to HIV/AIDS. The virus knows no national boundaries and was of significant concern to the state in the early years of the new millennium owing to the rising rates of infection among certain sectors of the population. The fact that most HIV/AIDS treatment, prevention, and education efforts in Barbados (and throughout much of the Caribbean) are managed and/ or funded at least in part through international agencies in coordination with national health organizations and institutions requires that any analysis of local HIV/AIDS discourses factor in transnational influences. Numerous scholars analysing the global HIV/AIDS pandemic have observed the ways in which the efforts of national governments and international health organizations to control and manage the spread of the virus often carry moral agendas that perpetuate long-standing gendered, sexual, race, or class inequalities. Researchers like Cindy Patton (1997, 2002), Paula Treichler (1999), and Thomas Yingling (1997) have demonstrated that, in the early years of the pandemic, media representations, government policies, and health organization interventions often further stigmatized the already marginalized social groups, ranging from Africans to female sex workers to homosexuals to struggling immigrant populations. In many cases, these forms of viral-based discrimination also reproduced the transnational racialized inequalities that were established during periods of colonization and are reflected today in ongoing political and economic inequalities between so-called developed and developing nations. Within the national borders of developing nations whose policies are influenced, if not dictated, by supranational organizations that control the purse strings of their

health and welfare programs, state-level HIV/AIDS discourses often reproduce these problematic moral agendas, and become a way of talking about or
constructing threats to the national body. The talk about ways to ensure public
health through prevention education often conveys moral agendas in which
certain bodies are privileged as model citizens of the nation state while others
are labelled as dangerous through their association with improper gendered
and sexual behaviour that renders them diseased and deadly.

My focus here is on Barbados's National HIV/AIDS Commission (NHAC),
which was established in 2001 'to coordinate effectively the national expanded
response to reduce the incidence and spread of the epidemic in Barbados,' and
whose mission is to 'advise the government on plans and policies and to build
strategic partnerships to effectively manage, control, and reduce the spread of
HIV/AIDS in Barbados.'[1] I focus on the ways in which gendered and sexual citizenship has been produced and defined, through analysis of statements made by
Barbadian government officials, publications of NHAC, and public discussions
about the work of NHAC in the early years of the new millennium. Much of what
I am arguing builds on Andil Gosine's research on the ways in which sexuality
rights and international development have been related through the AIDS epidemic. Gosine (2004) notes that while HIV/AIDS has resulted in recognition of
the importance of understanding sexual practices and customs in all aspects of
international development, and, at the very least, sexual diversity is now recognized as a universal fact, there are still significant problems in the ways in which
sexual minorities are perceived or represented in international development policies. For example, studies have noted that in many societies men have sex with
men as well as with women but in few societies is male-male sex widely acceptable. These studies often argue that in states where homosexual practices are illegal, laws must be revised so that there is less stigma attached to these practices,
allowing state health organizations to access this high-risk group better in order
to protect the wider society, because women are also at risk from these men.
However, Gosine notes that in places where same-sex sexuality is only publicly
discussed in relation to an HIV/AIDS framework, sexual minorities come to matter only in terms of causing or alleviating HIV/AIDS (2004, 5–6). This creates
or perpetuates a reductive understanding of the sexual identities of these groups
as something that is primarily associated with a dangerous disease, and therefore
also elides numerous other social and economic issues with which they must
deal. The end result is perpetuation of heteronormativity in development policy
and planning, which, once again, means that gender roles for men and women
are constructed within narrow confines (Gosine 2004, 10). In other words, HIV/
AIDS policies, which are now integral components of both national and international development programs, often reproduce dominant heteronormative frame-

works that are also colonially inflected racial and gendered frameworks, and thus contribute towards the privileging of a delimited gendered and sexed citizen of the state. Limiting discussions of same-sex sexual behaviour to an HIV/AIDS framework leaves no room available for thinking about sex in other, more productive and pleasurable frameworks or for recognizing the rights of men and women engaged in those practices.

Building on these observations, I argue that in Barbadian public and institutional HIV/AIDS-related discourses same-sex sexual minorities are, for the most part, unmentioned or unmentionable and that when they are visible, their visibility tends to be only in association with HIV/AIDS as 'risk' groups, thus producing a sexuality constructed solely in terms of being a problem or a threat. In other words, official and public HIV/AIDS talk in Barbados, while opening up new avenues of dialogue about sexual diversity in Barbadian society, has thus far re-inscribed normative gender/sex roles, privileging heteronormativity as the default foundation of 'good citizenship.'

Before I go any further, a few words are necessary to contextualize the place of homosexuality in Barbados. As discussed in the introduction, over the past ten to fifteen years the Caribbean has come to be identified as a homophobic region. In the previous chapter I reviewed media coverage on homosexuality in Barbados and found that it concurs with these claims; that is, I found a general pattern of negative representations of homosexuality in Barbadian media. However, as will be elaborated in chapters 5, 6, and 7, I also heard both gay- and straight-identified Barbadians claim that homosexuals are not discriminated against in terms of employment, housing, or general treatment because 'everyone knows' that there are homosexuals in positions of power and influence and no one is forcing them to quit their jobs. A number of gay-identified interviewees stated that there are members of their family, friends, and associates in their workplaces who are supportive and have no issue with their sexual orientation. At the same time, I collected stories of harassment and violence from other interviewees, many of whom stated that the situation in Barbados was not improving and they felt that there was an increasing amount of hostility towards them compared to that of fifteen to twenty years ago. Based on these preliminary observations, to claim that Barbados as a society (or the Caribbean as a region) is homophobic or discriminates against homosexuals is problematic because it glosses over complex sets of attitudes and values; it becomes a misleading appellation that obliterates the sexual diversity and acceptance of that diversity by many. As I will outline in subsequent chapters, there are complex and diverse widespread perspectives on same-sex sexual practices and identities in Barbados, so to claim otherwise is misrepresentative and forecloses further discussion of it.

Nevertheless, government departments and units like NHAC must develop policies in tandem with the laws of Barbados. Currently, there are laws in the Criminal Code of Barbados that are interpreted as anti-homosexual. These laws specifically criminalize acts of sodomy; strictly speaking, this means that heterosexual sodomy is outlawed as much as is homosexual sodomy. As some legal analysts have pointed out, it could therefore be argued that homosexuality is not illegal in Barbados, only certain sexual positions are, but in almost all contemporary discussions these laws are utilized as primary examples of the state's criminalization of homosexuality. The HIV/AIDS crisis was the catalyst for a parliamentary discussion and a government-sponsored report in 2004 that advocated for the decriminalization of the 'anti-homosexual' laws, which in turn generated a media frenzy.

Mia Mottley's Statement and the Walrond Report

In 2003, Mia Mottley, deputy prime minister and Attorney General of Barbados, spoke of the 'cancer of discrimination' that was preventing 'highly at risk' segments of the population from benefiting from HIV/AIDS prevention programs. She argued that the threat posed by male-to-male sexual transmission of HIV/AIDS to whole communities – a threat exacerbated by social discrimination against men who have sex with men (MSM) – compelled a review of the state's approaches to sexual regulation. A year later the Attorney General's office requested a consultation on the legal, ethical, and socio-economic issues relevant to HIV/AIDS in Barbados from Professor E.R. 'Mickey' Walrond, former dean of the School of Clinical Medicine and Research at the University of the West Indies (Cave Hill) and chairman of the National Advisory Committee on AIDS, 1987–94. His report recommended numerous revisions to Barbadian legislation relevant to HIV/AIDS, which were 'intended to remove the social barriers to the spread of HIV/AIDS' (Walrond 2004, 6). Once again, Professor Walrond recommended changes to the Criminal Code that would assist in the 'process of destigmatising marginalized groups such as homosexuals, prostitutes, and sexually active adolescents who are at high risk of HIV/AIDS infection, in order to diagnose them earlier and reduce the prevalence of HIV/AIDS' (2004, 7). Following the publication of this report, NHAC held a series of public forums in which they sought feedback on its recommendations. I attended three of these forums in 2004–5. Most of the comments addressed Walrond's recommendations to decriminalize laws against homosexuals and prostitutes and were vehemently opposed to any changes to the existing laws (I discuss the forums in more detail in the following chapter). The forums received a great deal of coverage on local television and in the two daily newspapers, the latter publishing a steady stream of letters to the editor expressing, for the most part, points of view that stridently opposed the report's recommendations.

HIV/AIDS and Homosexuality in Barbados

Mottley and Walrond's statements about homosexuality, HIV/AIDS, and discrimination were not just speculative opinions; they were based on studies of HIV/AIDS that were conducted by various groups throughout Barbados and the rest of the Caribbean. We need to keep in mind that throughout the 1990s and into the early 2000s Barbados had an HIV/AIDS prevalence rate of approximately 1.8 per cent (United Nations General Assembly Special Session on HIV/AIDS 2006), which translated to approximately 5,080 people living with HIV/AIDS out of a population of 280,000 (2007 estimate, U.S. Census Bureau, International Programs Center).[2] This rate was relatively high compared to that of countries like Canada (where the prevalence rate in the same time period was between 0.2 and 0.5 per cent), but significantly lower than that of other Caribbean countries like Trinidad (2.6 per cent) or Haiti (3.8 per cent) (Joint United Nations Programme on HIV/AIDS 2007).[3]

I found it difficult to obtain information on the modes of transmission of the virus for Barbados. One NHAC document stated that from December 1984 to March 2001, 86.8 per cent of HIV/AIDS infections had been transmitted via heterosexual sex, and only 5.7 per cent through homosexual or bisexual sex; the remainder were transmitted perinatally and via blood transfusions (NHAC 2001). However, as they note, these figures may have underestimated the rate of homosexual or bisexual transmission, owing to the stigma associated with these sexual practices. A more general, and perhaps accurate, statement about transmission can be found in the UNAIDS epidemic update report for 2006, which states, 'The Caribbean's largely heterosexual epidemics occur in the context of harsh gender inequalities and are being fuelled by a thriving sex industry, which services both local and foreign clients. Sex between men, a hidden phenomenon in the generally homophobic social environments found in this region, is a smaller but important factor, and unsafe sex between men is believed to account for about one tenth of reported HIV/AIDS cases in the region' (UNAIDS 2006).[4]

The Caribbean Epidemiology Centre's 2007 'Report on HIV/AIDS' in member countries makes a similar observation: 'As in the wider Caribbean, the primary mode of HIV/AIDS transmission in CAREC member countries is through unprotected sexual intercourse. In the early years, surveillance data revealed that transmission of HIV/AIDS was primarily homosexual; current data reveals a mosaic of homo/bi and heterosexual transmission with a current male-to-female ratio of almost one-to-one.'[5]

These and other reports go on to note that most Caribbean nations are homophobic and that their governments are unwilling to change discriminatory laws. Official indifference or hostility means that there are few prevention and care programs for men who have sex with men, which in turn means that these groups are not being reached and thus they continue to pose a risk for the spread of the virus among themselves and to others (that is, female partners).

Mottley's statements and Walrond's report were clearly influenced by this framing of sexual alterity in HIV/AIDS research. The positions argued that the rights of homosexuals must be assured in Barbados primarily in order to contain HIV/AIDS from spreading throughout the nation. This is a limited representation of homosexuality because it focuses primarily on men (there is no mention of women) who are constructed primarily through sexual practices, which therefore re-inscribes an old stereotype – the homosexual defined through deviant sexual acts – and adds another, more threatening layer: that these sexual acts are dangerous and may kill women and children. Thus we see an argument for the rights of homosexuals that is constituted primarily through devious and dangerous sex acts, which not only reproduces a problematic stereotype but also works to reproduce racializing colonial narratives about the 'natural' proclivities of non-white men and undermines the complex negotiations that they make in expressing sexual choices.

'Against the Laws of Nature'

Evidence of the ways in which the official recommendations worked to re-inscribe discriminatory attitudes towards homosexuality could be found in media coverage, particularly in Letters to the Editor sections of the daily Barbadian newspapers, *The Advocate* and *The Nation*. As outlined in the previous chapter, Alicia Smith's letter to the editor typified this type of response, emphasizing 'the disease profile and early death of homosexuals' in order to oppose homosexuality 'on purely medical grounds,' in which she focuses on the fragile male anus. She ended her letter by declaring the importance of maintaining 'our enduring Christian morality.'

Other letters similarly spoke of 'the abuse of the gift of sexuality' and/or the danger of legislating support for a sexual act that 'goes against the laws of nature.' In these comments, homosexuality was often reductively defined or discussed primarily in relation to a specific sexual act, anal intercourse, which came to stand for a particular type of person or personality type. The metonymic value of a sex act – standing for a deviant kind of person – illustrates the way in which this public debate over changing a couple of Barbadian laws[6] was about more than just decriminalization of a sexual activity; it was also about the way that the Barbadian state legislates the gendered and sexual identities of its citizens or, more generally, that the terms of citizenship are set in the Barbadian nation state. The problem here lies in the conceptual framework in which the terms of inclusion are negotiated, and how particular sexual practices and identities are organized to operate as the limits of inclusion or exclusion (Alexander 2005). In this context, there is one primary sign, male anal sexual intercourse, which represents and frames both sides of the debate over the homosexual's place in the Barbadian nation; the effect of this limited representation simultaneously re-inscribes long-established discriminatory attitudes towards those who are believed to engage in this act and now connects them to a deadly virus that threatens to infect the 'good' (heterosexual) citizens of the state. The result is to further 'abjectify' the category of the homosexual while simultaneously trying to 'destigmatize' him through decriminalization.

Defining 'Homosexuals'

Mottley's and Walrond's recommendations and the public reactions to them were often framed in terms of the rights of homosexuals: both *rights* and *homosexuals* are culturally specific and historically situated categories that need to be critically interrogated for the ways in which their meanings circulate in Barbados. The *homosexual* is a term with a Euro-American etymology; in most popular contexts it is a sexual-identity category in which particular sexual acts are tied to an essentialized identity, and this identity is presumed to have certain personality or behavioural traits. However, scholars of Latin American and Caribbean sexualities have demonstrated that using the label *homosexual* to describe a wide range of behaviours and values associated with those behaviours is problematic, and ethnographic research in these regions clearly demonstrates multiple, often fluid sexual behaviours and categorizations (see Kulick 1998; Lancaster 1992; Murray 2002; Padilla 2007; Prieur 1998; and Wekker 1999). While I met numerous Barbadian men who identified as gay or homosexual, some noted that there were numerous men in Barbados who had sex with other men and did not identify in this way for a variety of reasons, ranging from associating 'gay' with a metropolitan, middle-class, white male identity located mostly in Euro-American cities, to stating that they were primarily interested in women sexually, which therefore meant that they could not be 'homosexual.' In chapters 5 and 6, I analyse in more detail the way in which gendered and sexual roles, practices, and identities are articulated in Barbados, but suffice to say here that government and health officials who are advocating rights for and outreach to homosexuals may be only partially representing the sex-scape of Barbados and thus may be only partially successful in their desired social and health outcomes.

Furthermore, as noted above, the articulation of homosexual *rights* only in relation to HIV/AIDS prevention obscures a more complex analysis of the implications of associating sexual actions and identities with the state's laws and responsibilities, and their impact on the lives of Barbadian men and women. This will be discussed in more detail in the following chapter, but it is worth stating here that when HIV/AIDS prevention is the only focus, other consequences of repressive or negligent state laws are overlooked, such as issues of sexual harassment in public spaces (including workplaces), verbal and physical violence both at home and in the public, police harassment, employment discrimination, and other areas in which sexuality may be significant.

Conclusion

During the media melee that followed Mottley's statements and Walrond's report, I noticed that there were no comments or official responses in the media by any member of NHAC. I was not surprised. When I had interviewed a member of the executive board of NHAC in 2003 and asked what programs were planned or in place that targeted gay men or MSM, I was reminded that in Barbados the vast majority of transmissions are caused through heterosexual sex, but, more significant, the commission's 'hands were tied' when it came to outreach to groups like homosexuals and sex workers, owing to the laws of the Criminal Code. Members of the commission were well aware that outreach to these groups was critical,[7] but they could not make any public statements that supported more controversial proposals like changing legislation, which was a political hot potato; since they were funded through the Prime Minister's Office, they could not risk controversy.

Four years later, when I visited the NHAC website, I noticed that their motto, 'Stay Safe, Love Life,' was written around a red ribbon on every page.[8] While the website contained information on how HIV is transmitted, how to protect oneself, and where to go for testing or further information, there was no mention of sexual diversity, except for one line, which stated that 'men who have sex with men and commercial sex workers are examples of groups …[where] there is a higher prevalence of the virus because of their sexual practices, and therefore having unsafe sex with someone from one of these groups places you at a higher risk of contracting the virus.'

As one can easily surmise from this statement, the Criminal Code of Barbados remained unchanged; Mottley's and Walrond's recommendations were not implemented. More important, however, was the perpetuation of a reductive representation of a sexual minority to a (dangerous) sex act, and the deleterious effects of this representation on the place of homosexual men or MSM in discourses of citizenship in the Barbadian nation state, not to mention the perpetuation of the absolute invisibility of lesbians or women who have sex with women. It would be wrong to blame the Barbadian health and HIV/AIDS authorities alone for constructing and circulating this representation. As I have tried to demonstrate in this chapter, the Barbadian position on the relationship between sexual minorities, HIV/AIDS, and the state has been constructed in and through transnational discourses positing a particular set of values about the relationship between health, sex, gender, and the nation. While we cannot and should not dismiss the importance of targeting groups in public health programs who are at higher risk of contracting HIV/AIDS, a more meaningful public conversation about sexual diversity must be developed in order to recognize, guarantee, and protect the place of sexual minorities as equal citizens of their states. Until this conversation takes place, the interventions of the Barbadian state (and those of numerous other states both North and South) in the sexual health of its citizens will continue to perpetuate a message of heternormativity, which will in turn perpetuate the exclusion, marginalization, and dangerous silencing of significant numbers of men and women from effectively participating in their own health and well-being.

Chapter 3

Whose Right? Human and Sexual Rights Discourses in Barbados

As we have seen in chapters 1 and 2, there were a number of public forums in which issues pertaining to sexuality were being debated in Barbados in the early years of the new millennium, and the media were a primary site through which information and opinions were conveyed. Various governmental ministries and departments, ranging from health to education to gender affairs, also disseminated information pertaining to the social, ethical, and health-related aspects of sexuality. Churches represented a semi-public forum in which moral aspects of sexuality were discussed, and numerous non-governmental organizations, ranging from HIV/AIDS commissions to child-care boards to business associations to activist groups, discussed sexuality issues including policy development and agendas for social change.

Although chapter 1 focused on the primarily negative and critical opinions on homosexuality in Barbadian feedback media, there were additional public sites in which homosexuality was presented or framed differently. In a number of public and semi-public forums that focused on issues pertaining to homosexuality, the idea of 'sexual rights' was being vetted and interpreted in various ways. One of the first and most visible examples of the discussion of sexual rights in Barbados was then Attorney General Mia Mottley's attempt in 2003 to change certain laws in the Criminal Code that, as outlined in the previous chapter, were interpreted as anti-homosexual. In presenting her arguments for this change, Mottley said, 'While we would like to believe that there are normative values that will guide the society, the reality is that a government in a pluralistic society must accommodate and respect the human rights and the dignity of each individual ... To that extent, law, which seeks to discriminate in a society whose history has been scarred with the cancer of discrimination, has in fact to be reformed' (Karin Dear, *The Nation*, 12 October 2003).

A year later, a different interpretation of sexual rights emerged in the public forums organized by NHAC to elicit feedback on Professor Mickey Walrond's 'Report on the Legal, Ethical, and Socio-economic Issues Relevant to HIV/ AIDS in Barbados,' which was also introduced in the previous chapter. The report made numerous suggestions to address issues pertaining to HIV/AIDS; among them was support for the decriminalization of homosexuality in order to reduce the stigma and fear associated with HIV. At these forums, comments made by some members of the public indicated their interpretation of Professor Walrond's recommendations as support for the rights of homosexuals. However, in this case, rights were described in a different light. One audience member said that she could not understand why the commission was supporting the idea of giving rights to a group who engaged in activities of which most Barbadians did not approve. Another person spoke passionately about the need to protect Barbados against the 'gay agenda,' which was being promoted by a highly organized, secret group with members in positions of political and economic power around the world who were trying to force all nations to accept their 'gay rights manifesto.'

A final example of sexual-rights talk that revealed yet another interpretation of rights arose at a November 2004 meeting of United Gays and Lesbians Against Aids in Barbados (UGLAAB), a lesbian and gay support group based in Bridgetown. The topic for the night was discrimination against gays and lesbians in Barbados, and various people stood up to speak about their experiences. One of the members, whom I will call 'Pat,' described how he had been mistreated numerous times in stores around the city (either being ignored by staff or being told they couldn't help him with what he was looking for). He then pulled out two sheets of paper, telling us that he now carried around the Universal Declaration of Human Rights, which he had downloaded from the Web so that he could show people that he is equal and deserved to be treated with dignity and respect. Afterwards I said to Pat that the Universal Declaration of Human Rights does not include a reference to equal rights based on sexual orientation although there was a multinational movement currently attempting to revise the document to include this category. But that was not the point, he responded. 'What we need in Barbados is for people to recognize us as humans, not just gays. That declaration is about human rights, and I think we should be promoting *human* rights here, not gay rights.'

I will analyse below these different interpretations of rights, but let us first remember that claiming rights for particular groups is nothing new in that rights have been a primary route through which oppressed and/or marginalized social groups have been advocating change to social and political structures for over fifty years, with the civil rights movement in the United States often being considered the foundational model that all subsequent rights movements have followed (Goodale 2006, 1). Sexual rights advocates of many different persuasions in diverse societies have developed and built their strategies out of these earlier movements. However, in the above-mentioned examples there is evidently more than one way of understanding the meaning of *rights*. This chapter examines more closely the different meanings and their effects and how they demonstrate the different interpretations of sexuality and its social effects that are circulating through Barbados; these interpretations help to illustrate the complex and shifting terrain of sexuality (or shifting sex-scapes), which in turn both reflects and influences the changes in the relationship between the state and its citizens. I will also address the question of whether or not sexual rights discourses are the best way to advocate for social justice and/or bring about changes to social attitudes pertaining to sexuality in the Caribbean.

In particular, I will argue that framing justice and equality through rights talk may have deleterious effects for its advocates because there is no clear or transparent universality as to what *rights* mean, and particular interpretations may be used to further marginalize already stigmatized groups. I will suggest that it may be more efficacious for stigmatized groups (such as those who, based on their sexual practices, are not equal to their fellow citizens before the law) and their supporters to develop alternative strategies in which principles embodied in international human rights discourses are fused with local practices or performances that demonstrate similar values or logics, emphasizing justice, equality, dignity, and respect for all citizens. At the same time I will caution against the implementation of claims to rights based on unquestioned or unexamined local cultural traditions. This suggestion and cautionary addendum builds on Sally Merry's analysis (2006a, 2006b) of the multiple processes by which human rights are remade in the vernacular (local contexts), which may result in the further embedding of existing hierarchies of oppression (or the creation of new ones) while one works to erase them.

'What, Then, Is a Right?'

Judith Butler posed a deceptively simple question, 'What, then, is a right?' (Butler, Laclau, and Zizek 2000) in relation to an object of enquiry that we tend to assume is relatively straightforward in its meaning, but the closer one looks, the less clear it is in concept or practice. The examples presented above, with their different interpretations of *rights*, fit three of four categories put forward by Samuel Chambers in his article 'Ghostly Rights' (2003,149). The first way of understanding rights is as a demand for political and legal equality of all citizens of a state. Attorney General Mottley's reference to changing those laws that are discriminatory against a group of individuals and that result in their not being treated equally fits this interpretation. Mottley's statement reflects a basic liberal understanding of rights as guarantors of *individual* liberal freedom based on the *natural* equality of all human beings (2003, 149). As I shall elaborate below, a discourse of rights premised on the natural rights of the individual without clear recognition and delineation of the relationship between the individual, the social group (however the group may be defined – politically, religiously, culturally, ethnically, or sexually), and the state may be a naive, if not ethnocentric, approach to promoting equality and anti-discrimination for all.

The second way of reading rights is as *special rights*, that is, a demand by a particular minority group to be granted protected status or to be treated in some special way that will prove prejudicial to the majority. This interpretation can be found in the statements made at public forums on the Walrond report, when one individual said that she did not understand why a group should be 'given' rights when its sexual orientation was not approved of by most Barbadians; another spoke of how an elite group was trying to impose its agenda on Barbados, thus granting it a privileged position above the majority of Barbadians.

The third way of reading rights, according to Chambers, is that of *hegemonic articulation*, whereby a particular demand (that is, changing criminal laws) emerges out of the specific needs of a particular group but does so as part of a political battle that is dedicated to more universal projects or goals. It seems to me that Pat's comments at the UGLAAB meeting followed this line of reasoning. While Pat was very much in support of changing Barbadian laws that he felt were discriminatory, his reasons for supporting this change were not that his group (homosexuals) would gain special status or be recognized as a distinct group that was separate but equal to its fellow heterosexual Barbadians. Rather, Pat wanted laws and attitudes to be changed so that he would be treated no differently than were his fellow citizens when walking into a store. This may be extrapolating a bit from Pat's statements, but in line with Chambers' third category, one could say that this reading of rights is part of a project of radical democracy whose goals are more general in terms of the structural, economic, and political reforms that work to create equality across the social spectrum, without referencing or highlighting specific interest or identitarian groups.[1]

Universal, Cultural, and Individual Rights

One might think that official treaties or ratifications pertaining to human rights would reveal a more specific definition of what exactly the term means or entails, but this is not the case in international, regional, or national documents.

As numerous scholars have observed, within the language of human rights legislation there are tensions or contradictions that allow for different interpretations of rights like those described above (Cowan 2006; Cowan, Dembour, and Wilson 2001; Goodale 2006; Merry 2006a, 2006b; Sen 2004). In other words, these documents do not necessarily provide a clear definition of the way to resolve the competing or conflicting claims for rights, nor do they clearly explain how a nation state should decide who should 'have' rights and who should not when there are disagreements among different sectors of citizens. As Talal Asad has observed, universal human rights discourses are inherently hamstrung through their construction out of and against the nation state. While they espouse the equal and inalienable rights of the human family, responsibility and authority are under the jurisdiction of the sovereign state, which in most cases is also thoroughly invested in creating an exclusive national identity in each of its citizens; this in turn creates and perpetuates (again, in most cases) hostilities towards 'outsiders' or 'non-nationals,' with the result that particular groups reside within the jurisdictional boundaries of any nation state without the same rights as 'proper' citizens (Asad 2003, 137–8).

In addition to the universal or national tension that lies at the foundation of human rights discourses, a second, related tension lies in the understandings of and relationships between the ideas of public morality, culture, and individual freedom. As Jane Cowan has noted, culture has moved to the front and centre of rights discourses over the past fifty years, but 'culturalist claims might be used just as easily for reactionary as for progressive political projects' (2006, 10). Let me briefly touch on three such documents that are relevant to Barbados and issues of sexual rights in order to elaborate this point.

The first document is the Universal Declaration of Human Rights, adopted and proclaimed by the UN's General Assembly in December 1948. The declaration begins by stating, in article 2, that '[e]veryone is entitled to all rights and freedoms set forth in this Declaration without distinction of any kind, such as race, colour, sex, language, religion, political or other opinion, national or social origin, property, birth or other status. Furthermore, no distinction shall be made on the basis of the political, jurisdictional or international status of the country or territory to which a person belongs, whether it be independent, trust, non-self governing or under any other limitation of sovereignty' (www.un.org/overview/rights.html). Article 3 continues this theme of equal rights to every individual human being, as it states, 'Everyone has the right to life, liberty and security of person.' Article 12 uses a similar subject position, stating, 'No one shall be subjected to arbitrary interference with his privacy, family home or correspondence, nor to attacks upon his honour and reputation.' Based on these three articles, one might assume that in Barbados, if an individual felt that because of her sexual orientation her liberty, privacy, security, honour, or reputation were impugned, she could legitimately claim that her rights were not being respected and that measures must be taken to remedy this, because Barbados is a member of the UN and has pledged to honour the declaration. However, article 29 presents an important caveat: 'In the exercise of his rights and freedoms everyone shall be subject only to such limitations as are determined by law solely for the purpose of securing due recognition and respect for the rights and freedoms of others and of meeting the just requirements of morality, public order and the general welfare in a democratic society.' In this article the declaration refers to the *limits* of rights and indicates, albeit vaguely, that not everyone has the right to do and behave as they please. The declaration recognizes that there are laws in place to uphold 'morality and public order.' So if a person engages in an activity or behaviour that contravenes morality or public order, their 'right(s)' are constrained or overridden by the law. But, we might ask, who establishes what constitutes morality or public order? Who sets the rules? What if there are disagreements within a state as to what is moral and immoral?

In most cases, including Barbados, we know that establishing and enforcing rules regarding morality and public order are ultimately the responsibility of the state. However, when we think about this on a global level, we also know that different nation states have very different sets of ideas about what is moral and immoral, which are often tied to different religious, political, and/or cultural values; this in turn means that behaviours that are moral in one state may be immoral in another. Thus we return to Asad's point: a tension exists in the declaration between an assumption of a 'universe of free and equal humans' and the tacit recognition of different laws of different states, which may contain different ideas of who or what is morally acceptable and therefore may constrain or delimit freedoms or right to liberty (see also Markowitz 2004, 334).

The International Covenant on Economic, Social, and Cultural Rights, enacted in 1967, is an example of what is often referred to as the second generation of rights, emphasizing social and economic rights (Sen 2004, 319). This generation of rights documents introduces another organizing principle through a small but significant change in terms: whereas the Universal Declaration of Human Rights began by referring to 'all human beings' and 'everyone' being free and equal, the covenant's first article states that '[a]ll *peoples* have the right of self-determination. By virtue of that right they freely determine their political status and freely pursue their economic, social and cultural development' (www.un-documents.net/icescr.htm; my emphasis).[2] The subject is no longer all human beings as free and equal individuals, but rather all *peoples* having the right to determine their social and cultural development. In other words, there is a shift from the rights and liberties of the individual to those of the group and to its right to choose its 'cultural development.' The recognition of group or communitarian rights based on cultural principles introduces a very different set of premises upon which rights are to be established (Cowan 2006, 12–15).

When it comes to rights related to sexuality, the picture is even murkier because there is no reference to sexual orientation and/or sexual practices in the documents' lists of peoples against whom there should be no discrimination. One could interpret this absence to mean that discrimination against sexual orientation is acceptable, especially if one factors in the article 29 reference of the universal declaration to respecting public 'morality.' However, if there are people who feel that their security, privacy, and liberties are threatened, owing to a behaviour or practice that does not threaten the security, privacy, or liberties of others, then could they not argue that their individual right to freedom and equality is not being protected, and thus the state is in breach of its agreement to the principles of the universal declaration? Thus individual freedoms and public morality or cultural 'norms' sit in an uneasy relationship to each other in these UN documents.

The same tension between individual and cultural rights can be found in regional Caribbean documents as well. The CARICOM (Caribbean Community) Charter of Civil Society for the Caribbean Community declares in article II that 'States shall respect fundamental human rights and freedoms of the individual without distinction as to age, colour, creed, disability, ethnicity, gender, language, place of birth, origin, political opinion, race, religion or social class but subject to respect for the rights of others and for the public interest.' Article III claims that '[t]he States shall, in the discharge of their legislative executive and administrative and judicial functions ensure respect for and protection of the human dignity of every person' (www.caricom.org).[3] Thus far, the charter is similar in language to the UN's declaration, but Article X makes a more direct reference to culture: 'The States recognize that each culture has a dignity and a value which shall be respected and that every person has the right to preserve and to develop his or her culture. Every person has the right to participate in the cultural life of his or her choice.'

Once again, there is an inherent tension between the different sections of the charter. Individual rights and freedoms are to be protected by the state but are subject to respect for the rights of others, culture, and/or public interest, although in this case there is the addition of the right to choose one's culture.[4] In the end, the same question arises: what do we do if one set of people within a Caribbean state is claiming that its members are not being treated equally to their fellow citizens because of who they are or what they do, but another group says that the behaviour or practices of this first group offends its cultural principles or contravenes its interests? Is discrimination or inequality acceptable if it is inscribed within a cultural set of values? How do we define what a culture's values are? What if there are disagreements within a so-called cultural group about its values or what constitutes public morality or public interest? Is the answer simply, 'The majority equals the culture'? That is, if the majority of people belonging to a so-called cultural group claim that a certain behaviour or practice contravenes public morality, then an individual engaging in that practice or behaviour does not deserve the same rights and freedom from discrimination? In other words, does might make right? (Chambers 2003, 154) The problem here lies in an assumption that cultures are unchanging, bounded sets of traits and that everyone who belongs to a cultural group shares (or should share) exactly the same opinions, beliefs, and values. And even if such a definition of culture were true, then how does a state, with different cultural groups who are equal citizens but who have different ideas as to what is publicly or morally acceptable, decide which culture is right?

This tension of culture or public morality versus individual rights is at the crux of the debate about sexual orientation and rights, both in Barbados and in many other countries in and beyond the Caribbean region. Compounding the problem is that sexual rights have, over the past decade, increasingly been utilized as a symbol of unequal power relationships between developed and developing countries. As I noted in chapter 1, Matthew Engelke has analysed the way in which the government of Zimbabwe, under President Robert Mugabe, vigorously rejected international human rights groups' support of the rights of sexual minorities in his country, claiming that the language of human rights is imperialistic, disrespectful of national culture, and largely irrelevant to what it means to be human (Engelke 1999, 290). Engelke argues that it is problematic to speak about Zimbabwean culture as a singular, undifferentiated entity (he found a range of positions and understandings about homosexuality among the people he interviewed), but it is also problematic to speak about gay rights in a place where European or North American concepts of gay identity do not apply or carry different ideas about individuality, sociality, and sexuality.[5]

A similar reaction to international human rights groups who advocate for gay rights emerged in Jamaica in 2004, when Human Rights Watch (HRW) published the report 'Hated to Death: Homophobia, Violence, and Jamaica's HIV/AIDS Epidemic' (http://hrw.org/reports/2004/jamaica1104/). The report spoke of high levels of verbal and physical violence against men who have sex with men, and of general societal discrimination. It outlined a number of recommendations including reforming the law-enforcement system, repealing laws criminalizing sex between consenting adults, and revising the Charter of

Rights and Freedoms to include sexual orientation and gender identity in the sections addressing anti-discrimination. Following its publication there was an outcry from many leading figures in Jamaican politics, religion, and the media. The government attacked the report, telling HRW that it had no right to tell a sovereign nation what laws it should or should not have on the books. There were also strong denials of widespread discrimination against gays, and some argued that groups like HRW should first fix other problems in their own backyard, such as ongoing discrimination against gays in the United States (Williams 2004). However, it should be noted that the reaction was not entirely one sided. A number of articles and columns in the newspapers were sympathetic and supportive of the report and acknowledged that something must be done about the attitudes and actions against gays (that is, Maxwell 2004) but that pressure from international organizations may not be the best method for engendering changes in Jamaican attitudes and laws.

This hostile reaction demonstrates that the reports and activities of international human rights organizations are embedded in complex, historically inflected transnational, racialized, and politicized dynamics such that their reports are often read as representing 'white nations of the north or west' that are maintaining and imposing their power upon governments that supposedly are in breach of these rights. Echoes of these sentiments can be found in the reactions to the Walrond report in Barbados that were outlined in the previous chapter, where there were similar accusations that the author of the report was simply caving in to political correctness emanating from the United Kingdom and the United States, forcing Barbados to do something against the cultural will of its people.

Vernacular Rights

So, how can rights be negotiated? How can one work out the competing claims for or against a group's right to equal treatment or non-discrimination if international human rights legislation is contradictory, unclear, or in some instances interpreted to be hostile to a local cultural context? First and foremost, I would suggest keeping in mind Chambers' argument that rights are never natural or universal. There is a tendency in Western democracies to see rights as a 'transcendental truth': rights have always existed, albeit repressed or oppressed in other times and places, but democratic politics is on a march forward from less rights to more rights (Chambers 2003, 164), and the best framework for this process is a 'legalistic' one (whereby rights are instantiated in law). Chambers argues that rights are not natural but are in fact the product of political struggles and mediation and that they can disappear after they appear; there is nothing absolute about them.[6] Chambers says it would be better to think of rights as 'ghostly,' an idea that calls our attention to the vigilance and patience required to bring rights into being and to make sure that they do not disappear (2003, 165). Rights must be incarnated, and that incarnation takes place simultaneously through local political struggles and mediation across local, national, and international boundaries.

If we keep in mind that rights are ghostly, that legal frameworks are not necessarily the best or the only methods of implementing rights, and that the interpretation of rights discourses is located in local contexts of political, cultural, and social struggle, then how useful is the Universal Declaration of Human Rights? Michael Freeman argues that most societies around the world would agree to the declaration's basic principle of the inherent equality, dignity, and worth of every human being, and that the declaration can operate as a focal point through which groups or polities with differing value systems can meet to negotiate these differences; however, it is still problematic in its ability to provide specific guidelines as to how relations between peoples with different beliefs should be governed (Freeman 2004, 386). Freeman suggests that human rights laws must be determined through 'internal dialogues' that are generated by people from within a cultural or religious framework. He outlines how a number of Islamic scholars have been discussing women's rights through various interpretations of the Koran in relation to changes brought about through modernity (2004, 377–8; see Benyabib 2002 for a similar argument).

While the principle of internal dialogues is appealing, I think it is somewhat difficult to enact in practice. Globalization and its attendant transformations that are brought about through constant movements of culturally diverse groups across national and international borders, not to mention the ever-quickening flows of information and ideas communicated through electronic technologies like television and the Internet, mean that there are very few places in the world where we can speak of a culture unaffected by different value systems. Cultures, societies, and nation states everywhere are engaged in 'internal' discussions about social change, but these are brought about through contact with differing ways of being in the world that are creating changes in these local contexts. The internal dialogue is structured as much by what is happening externally; to put it slightly differently, the borders between what is external and what is internal are fuzzier than we might want to think. Furthermore, not all players are positioned equally in these internal domains, so that free and open dialogues may not always be achievable in practice (Cowan 2006, 17).

In Barbados I witnessed some people at the public forums and in the newspapers claiming that Barbados was a 'Christian' society or culture and therefore laws should not be changed to protect or give rights to' groups who transgressed or contravened biblically based values. In other words, if one argues for human rights to be negotiated through an internal dialogue that is based on cultural principles, then Barbados's human rights policies should be determined on the basis of a particular theology. This line of reasoning is problematic for a couple of reasons. First, while it is true that the majority of Barbadians identify themselves as belonging to a Christian denomination (according to the 2000 Population and Housing Census), there were eleven different Christian denominations, as well as 16,609 Bajans who identified themselves as 'Other Christians,' 1,657 Muslims, 2,859 Rastafarians, 1,293 belonging to other 'Non-Christian' denominations, and 43,245 people who listed themselves as having no religious affiliation (or at least none listed on the census) (Barbados Statistical Service 2000, 34). Therefore, if a Barbadian-generated language of human rights is to be negotiated based on a set of Christian religious principles, which one do we choose? What about those who belong to other religious faiths or who do not belong to any church?

Furthermore, a theological foundation of human rights sets in motion actions that run contrary to the principles of a democratic political system, which Barbados has adopted in its constitution. It states, 'No person shall be hindered in the enjoyment of his freedom of conscience ... [or] compelled to take any oath which is contrary to his religion or belief' (chapter 3, sections 19.1 and 19.5). In other words, the constitution states in several different sections that religious might is *not* necessarily right. Thus, the idea of an internal-dialogue approach to negotiating human rights may be easier said than done, for the culture of any nation state is likely to be a more complex affair, riddled with multiple interpretations of identity and morality that some members or minders of that nation state do not care to acknowledge.

Another direction to take in negotiating human rights can be found in Merry's analysis of how transnational discourses of human rights are adapted and/or transformed in local social settings. Focusing primarily on human rights approaches to violence against women, she outlines how human rights are remade in the vernacular, that is, the ways in which 'new' ideas are framed and presented in terms of existing cultural norms, values, and practices (Merry 2006b, 39). This is a difficult and complex process, requiring 'translators' who are critically important in the process of localizing human rights. However, as Merry points out, this process is not always successful; if human rights are presented as being compatible with existing ways of thinking, these ideas will not induce change (2006b, 41).

Following Merry, I am suggesting that sexually stigmatized groups and organizations develop alternative strategies in which international human rights discourses are integrated with local practices or performances that demonstrate similar values of justice, equality, dignity, and respect for all citizens. In other words, I am arguing that the ways to support claims for the equality, dignity, security, and liberty of all citizens can be found within the Caribbean social traditions and values that parallel the concepts communicated through international human rights discourses, but which may be constructed through different procedures (that is, not necessarily, or only, legalistic frameworks) and practices. This is absolutely and fundamentally a politicized process that would involve struggles over meanings because it is clear that there are also local practices and performances that work to promote inequality and/or ranking of people based on a particular practice or identity, as is clearly the case in issues pertaining to sexuality.

In the debate over sexual rights in Barbados and elsewhere in the Caribbean one of the first priorities should therefore be to reframe the parameters of the debate. The Walrond report, for example, has brought forward the issue of sexual rights under the framework of HIV/AIDS, arguing that it is important to work towards eliminating discrimination against those with HIV/AIDS as well as those groups who have traditionally been thought of as being at higher risk of infection; however, the commission notes that in the current climate all individuals are at risk and that transmission is now primarily through heterosexual contact. However, as I noted in the previous chapter, there are problems with linking the rights of sexual minorities to HIV/AIDS as it restricts the terrain of conversation about sexuality to one that is only related to the prevention of transmission of a deadly virus, which may reinforce negative stereotypes rather than alleviate them.

As we saw above, in Barbados, rights are also often debated through claims of discrimination or unequal treatment of one group at the hands of another. However, this too can be a complicated route through which to pursue social justice because there can be disagreement over what exactly constitutes discrimination, especially in the realm of sexuality. In Barbados I heard diverse opinions from both gay and straight people on the levels of discrimination faced by homosexuals. Some gay-identified men whom I interviewed told me that there are family members, friends, and work colleagues who are supportive and/or have no issue with their sexual orientation. However, I also heard about experiences of harassment and violence against homosexuals. Thus, to claim that Barbados as a society uniformly discriminates against homosexuals is problematic as it glosses over a complex set of attitudes and differing values and becomes a misleading appellation that obliterates sexual diversity and the acceptance of that diversity by many.

Returning to the possibility of developing a vernacular approach to sexual rights, we might begin by looking to other aspects of sociality or civil society in Barbados that emphasize respect and equality based on qualities other than, or in addition to, sexual orientation. These forms of sociality might be used as examples in the development or application of local practices and policies that protect and represent all citizens equally, including those with alternative sexual orientations.

One such form might be called populist egalitarianism. Anthropologists, historians, and other observers of Caribbean societies have observed that, especially among working and peasant classes, there exist various social mechanisms through which respect, fairness, and equal treatment are maintained. Examples of these mechanisms range from well-known institutionalized traditions of trade unionism and socialist democratic political organization[7] to more informal social mechanisms like humour, rum-shop debate, forms of entertainment like calypso and carnival or Crop Over, and even backyard gossip where neighbours often discuss and evaluate (sometimes ruthlessly) people who are thought to be exploiting others or treating them unfairly (Abrahams 1983; Jayawardena 1963; Mohammed 2003; Wilson 1973). In many cases, these performances or conversations work through disputes or show another side to stories, with the result that one might end up rethinking who is wrong and who is right or at least recognizing that things might not be what they first appeared. It seems to me that in popular culture throughout the Caribbean there is a long tradition of healthy scepticism towards people in positions of power, whether they be political, economic, or religious, especially when the powerful are preaching about morality and how people ought to behave. Thus it may be through these informal or popular forums that unfairness or mistreatment towards those whose sexual orientation is not standard heterosexual might be addressed.

One example of this approach came from an older woman who attended a talk on sexuality that I gave to a graduate class at the University of West Indies' Cave Hill campus in Barbados in February 2005. Afterwards, she told me that although she was a devout member of a Pentecostal church and had heard many sermons on the evils of homosexuality, she also had a neighbour who was known to be 'that way'; yet he was one of the friendliest people in her community, always said hello to her, and many times offered to walk with her to the store to help with her groceries. She said that, even though she had problems with 'that aspect' of him, she respected and valued him for his friendliness and kindness towards her, and she was now uncomfortable when she heard only negative things being said about these people in church.

I saw another example of popular egalitarianism in a theatre production in Bridgetown. *Pampalam* is an annual comedy show consisting of a cast of actors who perform skits in song and verse that satirize current trends and political events in Barbados. In their November 2004 performances, which consistently sold out over their two-week run, one of the most discussed skits in the newspapers and among my acquaintances featured two of Barbados's most famous calypsonians, the Mighty Gabby and Kid Site, who were dressed up in drag as bickering sex workers. When they first walked out on stage, the audience whooped and laughed for a good five minutes. The sight of these two well-known men dressed in spandex tights, with unevenly padded bras, dishevelled wigs, and badly applied make-up was clearly a visual joke because, as I was told later, neither of these men had engaged in a transvestic display previously and was not known for these kinds of antics. However, following the initial uproar, Kid Site sang a song in calypso style about being a sex worker working on the streets of Bridgetown and how 'she' found it quite interesting that all the politicians and 'big men' who condemned prostitution and proclaimed that it should be eliminated by day were the exact ones who came 'down from the hills' (referring to the wealthy outlying suburbs of Bridgetown) to visit her at night. As she sang, the laughter died down, and I saw people around me starting to nod their heads, and some responded to her lyrics, saying, 'That's right,' and 'She's right, you know.' The applause was a bit more subdued when Kid Site sashayed off the stage, but this was the song that seemed to garner most (favourable) talk in subsequent newspaper reports and the conversations I heard. This popular performance thus took a topic that was mostly condemned in the newspapers and by many politicians, and introduced a subversive perspective through a transvestic performance in a public arena that turned the critical gaze away from the prostitutes to those doing the condemning and asked indirectly who had the right to decide who and what is moral. While it may be overstepping the mark to claim that well-known figures in Barbadian popular culture like the calypsonian can single-handedly change public opinion in sensitive matters such as rights for sex workers or sexual minorities, the effects of their performances should not be underestimated and may, at the very least, introduce different interpretive spins on prevailing discourses of morality.

A final example comes from a comment made by a member of UGLAAB during one of its meetings. The topic for the night was 'stereotypes' of homosexuals in Barbados, but the conversation went on a tangent about how most of the members had not remembered hearing so much negative talk about homosexuality when they were younger. One woman, who was in her thirties, mentioned that she felt the increased popularity of dance-hall music from Jamaica was conveying to today's youth much of the hostile attitudes, yet she remembered being positively influenced by another Jamaican musical tradition, reggae, back when she was a teenager. 'I don't think Bob Marley ever said a negative word about homosexuality,' she said. 'I remember hearing his song "One Love" and thinking that it was meant to include everyone who loved everyone. That made a big difference to me then. What happened to that?' The other members in the room nodded their heads in agreement, and some began to name other uplifting songs they remembered from their younger days.

It would, of course, be naive to say that informal arenas such as popular music, *Pampalam* performances, and social banter are natural sites in which sexual diversity is celebrated, for these are the very sites in which one often finds negative messages about the topic. Furthermore, effecting change or support for sexual diversity requires shifts in other production sites of gen-der, particularly masculinity, and requires engaged activism from grassroots organizations. However, shifts in attitudes may be effected, bit by bit, through strategic, coordinated efforts between artists, community organizations, and governmental and transnational organizations that develop strategies empha-sizing fair play, respect, and justice for those who are mistreated for something that does no harm to others.

Conclusion

One of the main arguments of this book is that Barbados, like the rest of the Caribbean, is facing numerous challenges through rapid and major economic and technological changes, yet these changes and challenges are not necessar-ily all that new; for over five hundred years these societies have been forged through the transnational commerce of colonialism, migration of different ethnic groups, and exposure to multiple and often competing value systems. Homosexuality and homophobia appear to have been present in these socie-ties from their colonial inception (albeit in culturally inflected forms that have changed over time), but they have only in recent years become highly vis-ible indices of morality and social stability and citizenship in particular public forums and discussions.

Barbados is at a crossroads in coming to terms with its sexual 'others.' They are poised either to become the new pariahs among those unhappy with the current socio-economic situation, who strive to return to a mythic past of a communal, heterosexual, and homogenous (read *traditional Christian*) nation, or to become the vanguards of a new social order that recognizes sexual diver-sity and *the right* to sexual pleasure as a non-threatening element of a produc-tive, diverse society operating as an active partner in a globalizing economy.

I have suggested in this chapter that the answers to this dilemma are not necessarily or only going to be found in the language of existing international human rights documents or in the attempt to piggyback rights on the shoulders of the HIV/AIDS crisis alone. While I would not dispute that many aspects of social life in the Caribbean appear to be challenged when sexual diversity is presented as a matter of rights, perhaps if we emphasize the *equal* aspect of rights and tether it to, as well as develop it within, local contexts in which issues of egalitarianism and fairness are negotiated, then acceptance of sexual diversity and of equal treatment and respect for that diversity may grow.

Chapter 4

Gay Tourism and the 'Civilized' Homosexual

Up until this point I have primarily focused on how the homosexual is discussed in public contexts in Barbados. One notable characteristic of most Bajan public debates on homosexuality, whether they occur in the pages of the daily newspaper *The Nation* or in a town-hall meeting discussing gay rights, is that the homosexual is almost always an invisible figure, a ghostly haunting without flesh and bones and, most important, without voice. With the important exception of a few self-described 'out, loud, and proud queens' (*queens* is a local term with multiple contextual meanings but, broadly put, refers to effeminate gay men, some of whom dress and perform regularly as women; there will be more on this in chapter 5), the pages, airwaves, and public halls of Barbados are bereft of voices that self-identify as gay, lesbian, or homosexual.

This chapter and the following three chapters shift away from public representations of and discourses about the homosexual in order to focus on the 'invisible' (a term that I will partially challenge in subsequent chapters) lives of self-identified gay men and the more publicly visible 'queens' in Barbados. Too often, in much of the work on queer globalization and sexual rights there is a paucity of research on the lived effects of negative public representations of the homosexual, or we find that terms such as *gay* and *lesbian* are assumed to translate unequivocally to local contexts around the world. If I write that there are no gay or lesbian voices in (certain) Bajan public debates, what do I mean by *gay* and *lesbian*? Do these terms carry within them a Euro-American configuration that is produced through a particular arrangement of gendered, sexed, raced, and classed relations? Do *gay* and *lesbian* convey different meanings in a post-colonial society like Barbados than in urban North America? How and where do the more publicly visible Bajan queens fit into this sex or gender alignment? Who challenges homophobic discourses in Barbados, and how do they propose to eliminate them? What is life like for those who are the targets of homophobic discourses? Do they perceive their societies to be homo-phobic? Do they view themselves as gay or queer victims?

Through interviews, anecdotes, and stories by and about differentially posi-tioned, self-identified queens and gays in Barbados I attempt to show in these next four chapters some of the complexity of lives constituted through these dense local, regional, and global flows, inequalities, and interchanges. We will see that there is no singular identical definition of or position on sexuality, desire, or gender and their organization and operations in daily Bajan life. Rather, across these chapters we find similar intersections of local, regional, and globally circulating sexual identities that are structured and related through various raced, classed, and gendered hierarchies, as well as the centrality of the theme of respectability in Barbadian daily life and its complex relationship to performances of masculinity and femininity, which are in turn embedded in raced, classed, and heteronormative structures of inequality.

This chapter represents one possible point of entry into understanding eve-ryday gay life in Barbados: gay tourism. Gay tourism has been identified as an area in which new intersections of sexuality, identity, transnationalism, poli-tics, and economics are occurring. Yet, in some senses, it is nothing new. As Clift, Luongo, and Callister point out in their edited volume *Gay Tourism: Culture, Identity, and Sex* (2002), people whom we now call *gays* and *lesbians* have been travelling to various places around the globe for hundreds of years; indeed, historians are increasingly uncovering evidence that homosexuality was a common, albeit morally ambiguous, impetus to travel during the colo-nial epoch. However, over the past twenty years there has arisen a new niche in travel industries, mostly in North American and European nations, that focuses explicitly on consumers who identify and are interested in travelling as gays and lesbians, and this represents an important new development in the ways in which tourism, lesbian and gay identities, and knowledge about 'other sexuali-ties' are configured (Hughes 2002). One marketing firm has recently estimated that the American gay and lesbian community represents a US$54.1 billion travel market, or 10 per cent of the U.S. travel industry.[1] The International Gay and Lesbian Travel Association, founded in 1983, currently has over nine hundred members and publishes numerous travel magazines, including *My Gay World*, to its members. As niches go, then, this is one with substantial economic wallop.

Dean MacCannell argued in his now classic text *The Tourist: A New Theory of the Leisure Class* (1976) that the tourist is one of the best models embody-ing 'modern man in general,' a figure who allegorizes the tension between the 'present of modern society and its touristic outsides' (quoted in Giorgi 2002, 57). However, tourism today is a much more complicated thing; it is too complex and varied to simply represent one version of modernity, and some would argue that it has moved into a postmodern phase of multiple subjectivities and positionalities. The gay tourist is one such subjectivity that complicates this modernist construction, as 'he' represents an identification that was mostly marginalized and silenced in much of the dominant modernist narrative of the twentieth century. By marketing travel or holiday choices according to a sexual identity, we are witnessing in some sense a postmodern turn in tourism as it responds to a multiplicity of interests and subject positions. However, at the same time, some argue that, as an industry and an event, gay tourism is similar to its mainstream counterpart because it sustains social, political, and economic inequalities with very deep roots in the socio-historical firmament that we refer to as colonialism.

I want to examine the possibility that these modern and postmodern perspectives on tourism are partially correct but also incomplete; that is, I want to explore ways in which gay tourism complicates a standard modernist travel narrative that is built on rigidly gendered and heteronormative assumptions, but I also want to consider the ways in which gay tourism may re-inscribe other modernist themes of progress, liberation, and individual freedom that reinforce political and economic inequalities between citizens of Euro-American and post-colonial nations. In other words, gay tourism may complicate and subvert some of the dominant tropes of tourism as a social experience of modernity, but it does not challenge other aspects of modernity in its emphasis on difference and distance; it is still for the most part a service produced in and through Euro-American capitalist economies, in which movement away from 'home' and 'the everyday self' is marketed through the desirability of difference and/or distance, be it geographical, architectural, sensual, corporeal, sexual, or political. Furthermore, this difference between self and other is not valued neutrally but rather structured in an implicitly hierarchical relationship (Hall 1997).

Gay Tourism

In the following sections I will explore the situated production of difference and distance primarily through the comments of a member of the gay tourism industry in Barbados. Edward (a pseudonym) is a British born, gay, white male who is now a Barbadian citizen; he owned and operated a small bed-and-breakfast establishment on the island from 1998 to 2004. I found his B&B on a gay-travel website and stayed there three times between 2002 and 2004. During my first stay Edward gave me a presentation on 'the facts' of socio-sexual life in Barbados, and I subsequently noticed that he gave the same speech to any new guest who enquired about gay life on the island. I will examine Edward's speech in detail in order to highlight the way in which his representation of the Bajan socio-sexual terrain is deeply embedded in modernist hierarchies of race, class, nation, and colony. I will argue that Edward's comments resonate with the moral tropes contained within popular discourses of non-Western sexualities that are produced in Euro-American societies, in which 'other,' non-Western sexualities continue to be represented through contradictory characteristics of excess, degeneration, and unchanging tradition (Patton 1997; Lyons 1999).

Much of my argument is built on Gabriel Giorgi's engaging analysis of the literature promoting Madrid as an ideal gay travel destination. Giorgi identifies what he calls a 'globalized' politics of identity in gay tourism: 'The figure of gay and lesbian tourists "coming out" to the world combines travel and politics in an explicit way. Gays and lesbians traveling around the world as gays and lesbians reveals a map of democracies where it is increasingly conceivable to claim gayness as a way to move across spaces and borders. Gay tourism functions, in this sense, as an articulation between discourses of political rights and transnational displacements in a landscape where national borders are currently being reformulated in both their symbolic and practical effects. In this context, the gay tourist emerges as a cultural role, a persona that combines travel, social progress, and politics in new ways' (2002, 57).

Giorgi outlines the way in which the American and European mainstream gay tourism industry constructs a gay world: gay travel operators, guides, and websites promise to help the consumer find gayness in every nook and cranny of the globe. In this promise, however, there is often an implicit evaluation of these destinations: are they as progressive as 'we' are here in our democratic First World nations? Are local gays and lesbians (a cultural assumption about sexual identity in and of itself) as free as we are? In other words, gay tourism often produces a 'discourse of authority and witnessing that validates political progress, historical advances and dimensions of the visible in foreign lands' (Giorgi 2002, 58). The gay tourist, in a sense, becomes a flag bearer of progressive, socially visible gay identity connected to enlightened democratic nation states and is then used as the standard in evaluating the progress of non-Western societies.

Giorgi interrogates the ways in which Spain was marketed as a gay mecca during the 1990s. What emerges from his analysis of the literature produced by Spanish tourism authorities and gay travel books is a representation of a nation that has only recently discovered democratic modernity after spending many years under the yoke of conservative, oppressive fascism. The gay tourist's gaze, Giorgi argues, validates Spain as a now 'equal' player in the 'progressive' pantheon of liberal democracies and legitimizes the gay traveller as having a desirable identity and a rightful (albeit temporary) place in such a space.

Barbados differs in crucial ways from Spain as a tourism destination for gay- or lesbian-identified travellers. First, and most obvious, there is no effort on behalf of the Barbadian tourism authorities to package the island as a gay-friendly destination. While tourism is one of the largest industries in Barbados (Freeman 2000, 30), the ways in which it is packaged as a holiday destination tend to follow the well-established clichés utilized for much of the Caribbean; it is presented as a place of beaches, warmth, relaxation, and friendly locals who are excitedly awaiting the arrival of a North American or European heterosexual couple or nuclear family. Why there is no effort on behalf of Barbadian tourism authorities to encourage the gay or lesbian traveller can easily be surmised from the previous chapters, and I think it is safe to predict that it is unlikely that the Bajan tourism industry is going to switch gears and target what is now known as 'the pink dollar' in the near future.

European and North American gay travel operators and guides do not have much to say about Barbados either; it is clearly not a primary destination and receives cursory attention. Some gay travel guides, such as *Odysseus*, include a brief description of a nation's status on homosexuality, a practice that tends to impose evaluative, Amero-centric definitions of sexual identity, liberation, and politics; other guides simply list accommodations, restaurants, and clubs that are supposedly gay or gay friendly in Barbados; and still other guides contain no information whatsoever on Barbados. In the gay guides and Internet travel sites that I surveyed in 2002–3, when Barbados was mentioned, a couple of bed and breakfasts and hotels were consistently listed, along with a few restaurants and nightclubs. The B&B owned by Edward and his partner was one of these places.

Edward's Introduction to Barbados

There being so little information on Barbados available through gay-travel Internet sites and guides, the gay-identified traveller must find other sources to learn about gay life there. The appeal of a small bed-and-breakfast accommodation that advertises itself on gay-travel websites is obvious: the traveller assumes that he will have more direct contact with a local who has knowledge and experience of local gay life. Edward informed me that 95 per cent of his business came from gay and lesbian travellers, even though he also advertised on mainstream (non-gay) travel websites in Britain and the United States. He said that the lack of official advertising of Barbados as a gay tourist destination was not a problem for him because most gay travellers clearly had their own networks and methods for finding out about the gay orientation of a destination. Edward also stated that one of his main responsibilities towards his guests was informing them of 'the reality' of gay life in Barbados. Within moments of meeting me for the first time (in actual fact, moments after he had checked my credit card to make sure it was valid), he began to educate me about life on the island. He said that if I had come to pick up local men, then I was sure to be disappointed. As other guests arrived during my stay there, he did exactly the same thing.

Following is a condensed version of the remainder of Edward's presentation of 'gay Barbados,' which often unfolded in conversations over late afternoon drinks on the back deck of his home during the first couple of days after a guest's arrival. Edward would usually leave the initiation of a gay-related topic up to the guest because, as he told me, he could not simply assume that all his guests were gay and/or interested in gay life in Barbados. However, during my visits all guests (who were white men from either England or the United States) asked sooner or later if there were any gay bars and/or what gay life was like on the island. This would be Edward's cue. 'You have to be aware that Barbados is not like Canada [or wherever the guest was from];' he would begin. 'Here it is quiet and discreet. There are some beaches where at times you might be able to cruise a local guy, but if you are a visitor, it is unlikely you'll get any action as it takes time to get to know the Bajans.'

Edward would then mention that he was seen as different from the average white tourist since most local gay men knew that he owned property and lived permanently on the island; therefore, he was treated differently and had no problem in meeting men. However, he would remind us, he knew that many of these men were after him because of his money and not his looks, and he knew 'how to handle them.' This would lead him to warn us, the guests, to be careful of gold-diggers, younger black men who did not have much money and would only be friendly because they thought all foreign visitors were wealthy and would spend a lot on them. This 'fact' would appear to be borne out when I accompanied Edward to one of the local bars that had a reputation for having an unofficial gay night; more than once I saw what I assumed was a local, youngish-looking Bajan man go up to Edward and begin a conversation, following which Edward would buy drinks for both of them. Edward would confirm afterwards that the man was indeed a local whom he had not previously met, but he was sure that someone else who knew both of them had informed the man about Edward and what he had.

It does not require a great deal of explication to demonstrate how these kinds of statements and interpretations of local gay life convey a raced and classed framework that separates Barbadian men from Edward and the British or American gay tourist. Barbadian men were represented as belonging to an economically lower stratum than did Edward and his foreign guests, through his references to them as 'poorer' or as 'gold-diggers.' However, his presentation also conveyed racial difference: Edward would often substitute *black* for *local* as he would tell us how most 'blacks in Barbados were not well off, which is why some of the locals look for tourists.' This simultaneous pairing of local and black with lower socio-economic status would thus simultaneously render white as an invisible but powerful marker of the tourist's 'foreign' identity. This fusion of class-race relations resonates with long-standing colonially inflected binary representations of the poor, coloured, ignorant, not-to-be-trusted, sexually mysterious, and/or exotic colonized subject versus the educated, wealthy, and sexually and intellectually enlightened white Euro-American male.

This straightforward binary structure of socio-sexual difference was rendered problematic but was also reinforced in some ways by local gay-identified Barbadian men, some of whom did not frequent the bars visited by Edward.[2] Like Edward, most Bajans referred to the importance of socio-economic status in organizing gay social life, but they also identified important distinctions *within* Barbadian society. These will be elaborated in the next three chapters, but here is one example that illustrates the differences with Edward's representation. Omar, a twenty-one-year-old Barbadian who lived in one of the southern parishes and worked in a dry goods warehouse in Bridgetown, told me about a professional upper-middle-class social network of gay men that socialized in very different circles from those of the Barbadians who frequented the tourist bars. Omar claimed that his ex-boyfriend belonged to this 'professional class' of men who would have private parties in their homes and/or would travel to other international destinations for socializing and sex. Discretion was of the utmost importance because their professional status could be severely damaged or destroyed if their gayness were confirmed. Omar considered himself to be outside this particular class of men because of his age, job, and lack of income, but he thought he had appealed to his ex-boyfriend because of his youthful good looks (Omar's life story is presented in more detail in chapter 7).

According to Omar and others, there were Bajan men who did not circulate through the bars that Edward frequented because they could not afford the entry fees and/or the cost of drinks or they did not enjoy social spaces occupied by so many white tourists. These observations indicate a substantially more complex socio-sexual space, or set of spaces, operating in Barbados: gay-identified Bajan men emphasized or recognized differences of economic status in socio-sexual relations in ways that contrasted significantly with Edward's version. While some Bajans agreed with Edward's claim that poor black Bajan men sought out wealthy white tourists, in the Bajan version both parties were negatively evaluated; their depiction of this relationship emphasized the predatory sex tourist who came to Barbados to lure young men with money and other material goods, and any Bajan man who did pursue this kind of relationship was deemed not respectable. Michael, who was thirty-two years old and held a management position in a government department, told me that a number of gay Bajan men would not be comfortable in speaking with me in a restaurant or public place lest they be seen by other Bajans, who would think that we were 'involved.' As we will see in the next chapter, Michael's prediction was absolutely correct. Suffice to say that in self-identified gay Bajan men's descriptions of gay life in Barbados, socio-economic status and race operated in more variegated and complex ways than they did in Edward's narrative.

Another common topic covered by Edward in his introductory speech on gay life in Barbados was gay hang-outs. Edward would inform his guest that there were a few bars and dance clubs where, usually once a week, gay Bajans congregated, but this was never publicly advertised by the bar or in the media. Knowledge about these places was communicated through informal local networks, to which he considered himself to be connected. He would then list the dates and locations for the guest: Thursday night one should go to Ship Inn, Friday night to Harbour Lights Bar, Saturday night to Baku, and Sunday night to Ragamuffin. All the establishments mentioned by Edward were located in tourist zones of the island, and their clientele were mostly North American and European tourists (although a small but regular percentage of patrons were locals). Based on this narrative, one might assume that gay Bajans who were interested in socializing outside their homes would only do so in spaces that were not, for the most part, frequented by other Bajans, reflecting perhaps a desire to enter into a space of sexual liberation where one could feel free to be gay. Once again, after some time I learned from conversations with gay-identified Bajans that while this might be partially true, there were other reasons that some of them went to these bars; one reason was to prevent any rumour-mongering or gossip by other locals who might recognize them and wonder about the friends they were keeping. Also, for Bajan men who preferred white men, these were obvious establishments in which they might find what they were seeking. However, I would also be reminded that there were many Bajan men who preferred 'their own' (black men) and would therefore not bother to frequent these bars. Furthermore, there were other bars and/or dance clubs located around the island, with primarily local clientele, that these men sometimes attended, but such spaces were not known by Edward; this left his guests to assume that gay Barbadians would only enjoy and/or feel safe in a predominantly white tourist space. Edward's topography of gay space in Barbados once again conveyed an implicit racial coding by locating local (which, as mentioned above, could be read as *black*) gay men only in tourist bars, implying that they were aspiring to or desiring a model of metropolitan (white) queerness.

Edward's final comment on gay life in Barbados would be a reminder to 'be careful out there.' He would tell us that Barbados was, overall, a homophobic place, demonstrated by the fact that a few years ago one of his guests from the United States was beaten severely after he had noticed a local man looking at him on a side street in Bridgetown, assumed he was being cruised, and went up to the man to ask if he were interested in getting together. Edward said that it was common practice for Bajan men to look 'hard' at each other for a longer length of time than Europeans or Americans were used to, but that this did not necessarily signify sexual interest.

Edward was not alone in creating the impression that Barbados was a homophobic society. As the previous chapters have shown, the Caribbean is often presented in mainstream North American and local media as a uniformly homophobic space. One of the effects of these highly circulated discourses is to reinforce the modernist binary distinction between a modern, 'civilized' individualist and liberated Euro-American white society and an uncivilized, racialized 'other' through a disparaging portrayal of the sexual values and attitudes of the latter as culturally uniform, violent, and/or unjust (Puar 2007).[3] As I have already noted, this representation of a uniformly homophobic nation or region is deeply problematic for its tendency to erase what is in fact a diverse range of values and practices. As will be seen in the following chapters, while many of the gay-identified Bajan men with whom I spoke would agree that one had to be somewhat discreet in public domains, they did not paint a picture of a society that was uniformly or aggressively homophobic. Their descriptions of their own experiences indicate a more nuanced and complex social reality in which context, degrees of relationship, and personal politics mix in particular ways to determine whether or not sexual orientation is an issue, and that North American queer life, activism, and politics may not be the most appropriate framework for evaluating or changing the situation in Barbados.

Conclusion

It has not been my intent in this chapter to prove that Edward's overview of gay life in Barbados was entirely wrong; in some ways, I think his introductory comments to guests were helpful in that they revealed that homosexuality was not uniformly organized around the world and that one should not expect to find a scene in Barbados that duplicated a scene in London, Toronto, or New York. Furthermore, through his persistently 'queer' interpretation of spaces, people, and sociality and his portrait of Barbados as a gay space, or at least a space in which gay people existed, Edward produced a narrative that sub-verted the dominant gendered and sexual representations of Barbados found in mainstream media (and numerous social science texts) (Hughes 2002, 299). At the same time, his comments constructed and differentiated a normative pro-gressive, enlightened, wealthy, white, metropolitan gay sexual identity from a problematic, closeted, local, poor, black Barbadian one and, in so doing, re-inscribed a slightly torqued version of a long-established colonial narrative constituted out of ranked binaries of race, class, gender, and nation. While a society was being portrayed in which homosexuality was presented as hidden and in which local homosexuals engaged in socio-sexual relations for material gain, we were also being told in effect that Barbados was a nation in which homophobia operated as an acceptable hegemonic discourse and that this was a problematic attitude reflecting an ex-colonial nation peopled by poor racialized 'others' who were not as modern or as progressive as the people of the nation that had colonized it.

Edward's delineation of a society in which gay (as he and his guests knew it) regrettably did not exist echoes the Euro-American gay travel websites and brochures that cater to the growing numbers of gay-identified travellers who are looking for gay or gay-friendly accommodations, people, sites, and/or experiences. In these narratives and evaluations of the level of gay friendliness of a tourist destination lies the re-articulation and imposition of a particular nexus of historical encounters framed through race, economic exploitation, and political control. In the search for gay-friendly spaces or people around the world to affirm or reaffirm a modern gay identity and in the criticism of the lack thereof, a particular colonial narrative of inequality – what we might term *imperial pity* – is imposed on spaces and people who, for various reasons, do not comply with the self-titled configuration of the liberated, twenty-first-century North American or European gay man. In this sense, gay tourism is no different from the popular twentieth-century 'modernist' tourist narrative as it continues to construct and reproduce the distance and tension between metropolis and periphery, a universe in which self-described metropolitan gay travellers rearticulate colonially inflected cultural and racial hierarchies of rela-tions on a post-colonial map.

Chapter 5

Bajan Queens, Nebulous Scenes

In the first three chapters of this book, which focus on the consistently negative representations of homosexuality in public contexts in Barbados, I contended that the veracity of these representations could and must be challenged and that there was increasing documentation of the long-term and widespread presence of sexual diversity in the Caribbean (such as Glave 2008; Kempadoo 2004; Murray 2002; Padilla 2007; Wekker 2006). From my first visit to Barbados in 1998 until my most recent one in 2008, I readily found evidence of this diversity. In the previous chapter I presented one source through which I learned about gay life in Barbados, albeit a life presented from a modernist, racialized, and neocolonial perspective. However, it was not only through gay tourism that I was able to learn about queer life in Barbados. A few days after I had arrived on the island for the first time, my friend Joyce, a heterosexual woman in her sixties whom I had met while dating her brother in Washington, DC, in the early 1990s, introduced me to her dressmaker, Cynthia, who lived near her in a small home in a working-class section of Bridgetown. When I told Cynthia that I was interested in learning about gay life in Barbados, she replied, 'Us queens have been here forever, darling.' At that time, based on Cynthia's appearance and self-description as 'always thinking of myself as a lady,' I assumed that *queen* was a local term equivalent to the popular Euro-American sexual term *transgender* (male to female). Cynthia was well known on her street, and neighbours would often drop by or shout, 'Hello!' through her open window as they passed by during our chats.

On a subsequent visit in 2002, I began to see references in the local newspapers to a group named United Gays and Lesbians Against AIDS in Barbados (UGLAAB). I met and interviewed the founder and president at that time, Darcy Dear, who described how he had owned and managed a bar in Bridgetown for 'queens, gays, and lesbians' that had been in existence for at least twenty years. Owing to the increasing challenges and problems brought about by the HIV epidemic, she[1] had felt compelled to start up UGLAAB, which was dedicated to supporting people with HIV/AIDS and educating Bajans about the virus. Throughout our conversations Darcy would interchangeably refer to himself as gay or a queen, which confused me at the time based on my understandings of these terms derived through my experiences as a white, North American, gay-identified male. In North America gay and transgendered communities are popularly thought of as distinct groups based on their different sexual and gendered orientations (Valentine 2007). At that time I thought Darcy's usage of these terms indicated the possibility of at least two or more queer communities existing in Barbados, transgender and gay or lesbian, and that perhaps she was telling me that she felt comfortable in both groups.

During that same visit, one afternoon as I was walking down Broad Street, the main commercial avenue of Bridgetown, I passed a high-end jewellery store and saw behind the counter a person whom I assumed to be male, judging from his outfit, a suit and tie; however, the suit was bright red, the tie was an iridescent blue, and a multicoloured silk scarf was artfully arranged in the breast pocket. Furthermore, this 'male' was clearly wearing make-up. Through Darcy, I discovered that this was Didi, another self-identified queen, who later told me that she was 'well known to everyone' because she and two other queens did weekly drag shows at hotels and bars around the island, and she was also the multiple-award-winning flag bearer of a Kadooment band (street band) for the annual Crop Over festival, Barbados' equivalent of carnival. Didi became the president of UGLAAB in 2003 and was often quoted in newspaper articles discussing HIV and gay-related issues.

However, it would be wrong to assume that these queens' visibility in working-class neighbourhoods, commercial streets, hotels, media, and support groups translates to a social environment celebrating sexual diversity. As I will discuss in more detail below, discrimination and harassment, ranging from the denial of housing to verbal epithets and physical violence, are part of everyday life for many queens, and several feel that life in Barbados has become more difficult for them over the past twenty to twenty-five years. Nevertheless, the presence of queens (some of whom also refer to themselves as gay) in the public culture of Barbados was notable, and certainly rendered problematic any depiction of uniform regional homophobia.

This Bajan sex-scape was also notable for the almost complete absence or invisibility of what I would label *gay men* in public, activist, and/or community-leadership domains. Put slightly differently, I became curious about the absence of self-identified gay men – based on my Euro-American definition of *gay* as gender-normative males with same-sex desires – in Bajan public culture. While I met numerous self-identified gays and lesbians who attended the UGLAAB meetings, Darcy's bar in Bridgetown, and semi-private parties around the island, most were discreet and carefully managed their bodies, clothing styles, and language in ways that conformed to gendered and heteronormative standards in public domains such as the street, workplace, and school. While Darcy and Didi were quasi-regular figures in the newspapers and were often identified as representatives of Barbados's gay community, not once did I see a photograph or name of a gender-normative gay man or lesbian. While the occasional letter to the editor, a column, or a caller on a radio talk show would support gay and lesbian rights, most would be done anonymously or would clarify the person's sexual orientation as heterosexual or avoid any reference to his or her own sexual orientation.

Thus, it appeared that queer activism in Barbados was facing a challenge directly inverse to that of queer communities in North America. While the latter have made significant progress in achieving lesbian and gay rights and becoming accepted in public domains and institutions, transgendered people are still struggling to be accepted as equals within both the wider society and the queer community. In Barbados it initially appeared to me that transgendered individuals had achieved greater public acceptance or, at the very least, were more publicly visible and that they were at the forefront of queer community organization and activism; lesbians and gays, however, appeared to be the 'problematic' group that was less socially acceptable and visible and was not as well integrated into the queer community of Barbados. Thus, the obvious question seemed to be how and why this situation had come to exist in Barbados. How and why were transgendered people visible and relatively socially accepted in public culture while gays and lesbians remained relatively invisible and problematic?

But what if I am asking the wrong question or at least setting up the question with a series of problematic assumptions? What if my definitions of *gay* and *transgender* are not synonymous with those of the Bajans who describe themselves as gay and queen? What if Bajan sexual diversity or the Bajan sexscape is organized in ways that partially overlap or are co-constitutive with hegemonic queer Euro-American discourses of identity, community, and activism, while its practices and identities are refracted through other discursive sociocultural, political, and economic influences generated locally and transnationally? In the rest of the chapter I pursue this possibility, arguing that while sexual diversity in Barbados is immersed in, partially productive of, and produced through contemporary Euro-American gendered and sexual politics and identities (which are produced and circulated through mobile bodies of tourists, workers, lovers and relatives, communication technologies, and liberal democratic political and economic policies), this diversity is simultaneously produced through and in relation to local and regional gendered and sexual identity politics. Such politics requires us to acknowledge the ongoing influence of a colonized past and its attendant classed, raced, and cultural dynamics that produce unstable, unpredictable, and multiple possibilities of sexual subjectivities. I argue that this sex-scape is neither an illustration of a creolized or hybrid culture nor a reflection of a pluralistic compendium of multiple, discrete cultures, since both of these theoretical approaches risk oversimplification, as noted by Slocum and Thomas in their excellent historical review of Caribbean anthropology. These approaches tend to emphasize either separate, unintegrated cultural communities existing alongside each other (pluralism), implying an incompatible and dysfunctional sociocultural system, or the way in which Caribbean societies have produced a singular culture that seamlessly blends together the influences of their diverse ethnic and racial backgrounds (creolization), thus often obscuring ongoing significant cultural, class, and racial hierarchies (Slocum and Thomas 2003; see also Palmie 2006).

Rather, I suggest that some queens' understanding of themselves as queens *and* gay, their controversial visibility, and the relative public invisibility of gays and lesbians reflect subjectivities and positionalities that are produced through an ongoing tension between differentially located and performed subjectivities and values. The latter are pieced together in myriad contextually shifting ways by individuals who are marginalized by virtue of their non-heteronormative desires and identifications, resulting in contextually produced, potentially multiple subject positions (albeit within limits imposed through economic, racial, gendered, and other structures of inequality). This argument is influenced in part by Tom Boellstorff's notion of 'dubbing culture' to explain the formation of contemporary Indonesian 'lesbi and gay' subjectivities (2003). Dubbing culture challenges the 'global gay' argument that posits that traditional sexual cultures, mostly located in the developing world, are adopting Euro-American gender-normative gay and lesbian sexual identities. Boellstorff's analysis emphasizes that Indonesians have learned about these identifications primarily through the international media but have reworked them as they adopt them for themselves. The dub concept is taken from the filmic process whereby a film's original soundtrack is replaced by a version in another language, resulting in a juxtaposition where speech and gesture never fully match: 'the seams show' (2003, 236). Gay and lesbian Indonesians are thus engaged in a process of bricolage that cannot be fully defined or conceptualized in terms of traditional origins, because neither the origins nor their outcomes are ever fully stable.

While Boellstorff focuses on the ways in which dubbing culture can be productively applied to thinking through the influence of Western sexual subject positions in non-Western places, the Barbadian sex-scape differs in one crucial sense: it has never not been Western. In fact, as many have noted, it may be considered to be part of a region that is the crucible of Western modernity as we know it today (Abdur-Rahman 2006; Kempadoo 2004; Slocum and Thomas 2003). Furthermore, as Aliyyah Abdur-Rahman argues, we cannot understand modern Western epistemologies of sexuality without acknowledging their co-formation with racial theories that support the coercive regimes of race-based social stratification deployed throughout colonial empires (2006, 223). In other words, the homosexual and the heterosexual, and their deeply gendered characteristics, were and are defined by and through whiteness, blackness, and the various ethno-racial categories in between. Thus, a person like myself who is identified as a middle-class, gay, white academic male living in present-day Toronto is embedded in a socio-historical process that results in deeply different positions of privilege and power but does not render him any more or less 'authentic' in his sexual subjectivity than a person who defines herself or himself interchangeably as a queen and gay in a working-class neighbourhood of Afro-Caribbean people in the Caribbean. At the same time, I emphasize that a key difference that Barbadian same-sex cultures present to Euro-American queer hegemonies is located not in or through their violent marginalization (though this may occur) nor in their cultural difference from Euro-American queer communities (although there are differences), but rather in the racialized subjects who inherit white supremacist heteropatriarchal colonization as a frame for their identities. Barbadian participants in same-sex sexual cultures are structurally aligned with queers of colour, indigenous queer, and two-spirit people in North America in ways that destabilize the ability of Euro-American queer studies or Western sexual rights discourses to explain them. These insights build on the critique and reorientation of queer scholarship that has been generated by queer of colour, queer diasporic scholars, and queer indigenous scholars including Roderick Ferguson (2004), Juana Maria Rodriguez (2003), Daniel Heath Justice (2006), David Eng (2001), E. Patrick Johnson and Mae Henderson (2005), Martin Manalansan (2003), and Rinaldo Walcott (2003). Finally, David Valentine's (2007) insightful analysis of how the gay-transgender split is classed and racialized in America and how working-class queers of colour complicate these hegemonic sexed and gendered classifications provides important parallels with Barbados and has also influenced my analysis of conversations and interviews with Bajan queens and gays.

My objectives in the remainder of this chapter are thus threefold: (1) to provide a brief (and only partial)[2] description of the complex socio-sexual terrain of Barbados, primarily from the perspective of Bajan queens; such documentation is necessary given the relative paucity of ethnographic research that currently exists on diverse sexualities in the Caribbean (Kempadoo 2004, 44; Reddock 2004) and indeed throughout the African-American diaspora (Ferguson 2007); (2) to analyse how and why a particular sexual subject position – the queen – appears to·occupy a relatively accepted and visible position in Bajan public culture while gay-identified individuals are apparently invisible; and (3) to analyse how and why Bajan sexual subjects like gays and queens do not mirror Euro-American sexual subjectivities and their relationships to hegemonic socio-sexual values. Particularly relevant to the Bajan sex-scape are racialized intersections of gender and class structured through discourses of respect and reputation, albeit in ways that challenge Wilson's (1973) seminal formulation of these concepts.

'Almost Every Neighbourhood Had a Queen'

'Almost every neighbourhood had a queen,' said Cherry, one of the members of a drag show troupe who performed in hotels and bars around the island. In my interviews with Cherry and other self-identified queens I would ask if they remembered seeing or hearing about individuals similar to themselves when they were growing up. Cherry, who was in her mid-thirties, told me that she grew up in a number of 'middle-class' neighbourhoods around Bridgetown with her mother, who worked in the civil service, and her father, who was a school teacher, and that there was always a queen to be found wherever she lived: 'When I was in private school, there was a queen who used to make all the kids' clothes.' Divina, another member of the drag show troupe, did not remember seeing any queens in her self-described 'upper-middle-class' neighbourhood, but she remembered hearing people talk about 'men that dress up,' whom they'd call *she-she* or *bullers*, and then seeing them every year during Crop Over: 'They had their own Tuk band, and I remember everyone in the crowd talking about "the buller band," waiting for them to come down the street with their costumes, make-up, and feathers ... I was terrified of them but also fascinated by them. Drag queens were fierce then; you could not look at them too hard or they would stab you.'

Darcy and Didi also remembered the queens in Crop Over parades during their childhood, but Darcy, who is now in his fifties, remembered an even bigger event that attracted a great deal of attention, the Queen of the Bees pageant. This annual affair was held at different venues, ranging from the Globe Theatre (a movie cinema located near the Queen Elizabeth Hospital in Bridgetown) to its most memorable site, the National Stadium, where, Darcy told me, 'thousands of people, both gay and straight,' attended. Other older queens (mostly in their fifties and up), as well as older heterosexual Barbadians, ranging from university professors to residents of Bridgetown, also remembered hearing or reading about the pageant, and many noted that it was the type of event that members from all levels of society attended. According to Darcy, this was 'an event to be seen at,' and everyone attending, from queens to straight people, dressed up in their finest clothes for an evening of entertainment and socializing.[3] Darcy said that the pageant reached its peak in the 1970s but went into decline once the AIDS epidemic hit the island in the mid-1980s, along with the rise in popularity of fundamentalist Christian churches.

Mr Lovelace, an older self-identified gay man in his seventies, also remembered the pageants, but in his neighbourhood, near Eagle Hall, he preferred to attend regular semi-private parties for men that were held in a rented room in a private building or in the yard behind someone's house. These parties were attended by mostly married men 'who had a grand time with each other,' according to Mr Lovelace, indicating that there was a separate spectrum of less public social events for more gender-normative men who desired men. 'Everybody [in the neighbourhood] knew what was happening at those parties,' he added, 'but no one fussed.'

Most of the queens spoke of a mother, auntie, or grandmother who 'knew and understood' who and what they were when they were growing up. Divina said that her mother and aunt would 'kill for me' if anyone threatened or harassed her, and some queens noted that their fathers, stepfathers, or male relatives were also supportive but cautioned them 'to be careful out there' (Gigi). However, Darcy told me that over the years she had sheltered young queens who had been thrown out of their homes by their family, once again indicating that there was uneven acceptance of non-normatively gendered individuals in communities around Barbados. Darcy said that the older queens would look out for and protect the younger ones 'coming up,' would give them advice, and would provide them with a roof over their heads as well as other forms of material and economic support if necessary.

In the working-class Bridgetown neighbourhood where Darcy's bar had been in operation for at least twenty years, I was informed that most people (male and female) had their best clothes made by queens and that some queens ran rum shops, which were frequented regularly by heterosexual men, while others operated small convenience stores, out of a room at the front of their home. Joyce, who grew up in this neighbourhood, said that everyone knew the queens, and while the children would often make jokes about them to each other, they would never dare to directly taunt a queen: 'They were fierce and got respect.' Many of the queens' tales of yesteryear also included memories of being verbally harassed as youngsters; name calling, such as *buller*, *she-she*, or *girlie*, in school yards and on the street was a common occurrence, but most added that this was not accompanied by the threat of physical violence. Gigi, a younger queen in his twenties, said he was never 'bashed' growing up, although he would 'talk back hard' and confront his harassers. Fierceness through talking hard or fighting back and getting respect were qualities of the queens that were repeated by other interviewees, which I eventually understood to be indicative of a particular calculus through which gendered and sexual diversity was organized and evaluated in these neighbourhoods. Cherry summarized it most succinctly: 'There were a lot of people who were very, very tolerant, but, once again, what they were looking for is how you carry yourself. If you are common … you will be treated that way. If you carry yourself in a certain way, the respect you will be carrying, you would get the respect of your peers; so it's a trade off.'

What emerges from Cherry's comments are Peter Wilson's classic Caribbean social referents of respectability and reputation negotiated in and through local public and semi-private domains such as the street, yard, shop, and holiday celebrations. Cherry notes that a queen could earn respect from her peers through the way she 'carried' herself, which encompassed not just bodily comportment but also behaviour towards and treatment of fellow community members. Yet equally important was a queen's reputation for being fierce and standing up to anyone who confronted her; therefore, the respect was also derived from having a fierce reputation.

As noted in the numerous critiques of Wilson and the debates over the organization, arrangement, and salience of respect and reputation as a primary organizational structure of Caribbean sociocultural life, it is deeply problematic to assume that respect or reputation can be achieved by or applied to only one class, race, age group, or gender (Freeman 2007, 5–6; Slocum and Thomas 2003, 556; Thomas 2004, 5–6; Whitehead 1997, 422–3).[4] Chevannes's research on the role of the street in the socialization of poor, urban Jamaican males emphasizes that the street is interpreted to be the primary site where reputation is learned; it is a male space where toughness is learned, and it is the site of heterosexual initiation (2003). Stories of growing up in Bridgetown conveyed similar elements of toughness on the street, where boys who did not act in an appropriately masculine way were insulted and harassed, but I think it is notable that these stories also included memories of queens walking the streets, running shops, and participating in public celebrations in which they interacted, confronted, worked, and partied with fellow community members. Through a combination of having 'respectable' behaviours (running a business, looking after family members, treating neighbours courteously, not flaunting private relationships in public, not being a gossip) and having a reputation for talking 'hard' (see Abrahams 1983) or fighting back if they were challenged or insulted, these queens were engaged in and practised a set of values, an ethos, or calculus of worth that other members of these mostly working-class communities shared, which transcended or at the very least repositioned gendered and sexual dispositions so that they were not the only or primary features through which an individual was identified and evaluated. I will return to this point below and in the concluding chapter, but suffice to say at this point that from the queens' stories of life in Afro-Barbadian communities up to the mid-1980s, a picture emerges of gendered and sexual diversity that was visible and at the very least acknowledged, if not unequivocally accepted in everyday life.

Queens and Gays

As noted above, most queens felt that they were more accepted 'back then.' This opinion emerged through the memories of queens in their fifties or older, such as Darcy and Cynthia, and in the conversations of younger queens like Divina, Didi, Cherry (all in their thirties) and Gigi (twenty-six) who would remember stories and experiences of older queens and compare them with their lives today. Explanations abounded as to why attitudes had changed, but the most common factors noted were the rise of the HIV/AIDS epidemic throughout the 1980s, the increased popularity of fundamentalist churches (Pentecostal, Wesleyan, Evangelical, Seventh-day Adventist), and the increasing popularity of Jamaican music, specifically dance hall in the 1990s, with its aggressively hetero-masculine, misogynist, and homophobic lyrics. Darcy had to close her shop in the late 1980s and leave the island for a few years as her friends started to 'drop off' from AIDS, and rumours spread that AIDS could be caught from that shop. When she returned in 1999, she took over a bar that had been run for many years by a gay couple who had both died of AIDS. Darcy said that the bar became a refuge for queens, gays, and lesbians who were forced into hiding because of people's fear and ignorance of the virus. This discrimination against and suffering of her friends and patrons motivated her to organize UGLAAB and hold an official public launch in National Heroes Square (located in downtown Bridgetown) on World Aids Day in 2001. Although there was some controversy surrounding the launch, Darcy maintained that the group was welcomed by the minister of health and the director of the newly formed National HIV/AIDS Commission.

Many of the queens felt that an additional problem today was a lack of support and mutual respect between gays and queens, but there were diverse explanations of the basis of and reason for these divisions. Some, like Gigi, identified 'malicious gossip' as the primary reason he could not trust his fellow gays: 'When you see it comes to that mouth, and that red carpet unrolls, and they speak with that big trumpet of a mouth, they can destroy you, you know?' He felt that other gays were jealous of him because of his success in the fashion design business at a young age. Gigi also felt that a lot of men who were bisexual or 'on the down-low' (keeping their desire for men and their sexual relationships with them a secret from family and workmates) 'don't want any gays around them because we are openly gay people who feel comfortable with our sexuality.' Gigi's comment introduced a distinction between those who are openly gay and other categories of bisexual or down-low men, which I did not hear mentioned in the stories of yesteryear, although there was often mention of the need to be discreet. Other queens such as Didi and Cherry emphasized the lack of mutual support between themselves and gays and felt that they were the ones doing most of the work of supporting and defending the community against hostile public opinion.

What I found interesting and confusing in these discussions were the ways in which individuals would employ various combinations of gendered and sexual identity terminologies to describe themselves and the sex-scape of contemporary Barbados. As noted above, the range of terminologies and divisions through which gendered and sexual desires were identified, organized, and compared seems to have proliferated in the talk about contemporary Bajan socio-sexual life compared to that of yesteryear. One of my first interviews took place with Cherry, whose analysis of the problems faced by gendered and sexual minorities in contemporary Barbados was, to me at that time, articulate and easy to comprehend:

CHERRY: A lot of the gay people have lost respect in themselves ... because of the way they carry themselves.

DAVID MURRAY: Are they rude to you?

CHERRY: Yeh, yeh, yeh. Some of them are rude, bombastic, uneducated; there is a whole list of negativities that some of them carry, and they carry them with glee.

DAVID: So, like, why have gay guys become more disrespectful to themselves and to others?

CHERRY: I think lots of gay men have seen that queens have actually been more accepted than gay men ... I think that lots of queens here can do things and go places and get away with stuff that a gay man would get a bit of a tongue-lashing for.

DAVID: If people found out he was gay?

CHERRY: Yeh. [We] are totally out there, we have nothing to hide, our life is an open book. But you've got somebody now who is in the closet, got the family, the kids, and all that stuff, and they've got a lot to lose ... so they avoid many things, and you find they actually avoid queens.

DAVID: That's kind of sad.

CHERRY: Yes, that is sad, because wherever we go we don't just push queens, we push gay people first, and we take it to a deeper level.

Throughout most of our interviews Cherry maintained a relatively clear distinction between queens and gays, and I found her descriptions of the two groups relatively easy to comprehend because they reflected my understandings of the transgendered-gay divide in North American mainstream queer culture. Cherry described herself as transgendered and in the process of transitioning from male to female; so her body was 'coming into balance' with her mind, in which she'd always known she was a girl. Growing up, she said, she never thought of herself as being gay although some people considered her to be that.

Divina also defined herself as transgendered and used the term *queen* to describe herself in our conversations; like Cherry, she said that she had grown up feeling like she was a girl trapped in a boy's body, and she had always dreamed of being 'a living black Barbie.' Yet a few minutes after telling me this standard (according to my perception) transgendered line, Divina described how, when she was seventeen, the pastor at her Pentecostal church had tried to cure her of her 'sickness' by telling her that God would punish her by giving her AIDS, which she found strange because 'I never told him I was gay.' She went on to discuss how 'as a gay person you face so many obstacles … so it is important to find a path to spiritual enlightenment.' Divina's array of sexual identity terms in our conversations confused me because I assumed that a male-to-female transgender person would not describe herself as gay since the latter term, according to my Euro-American definition, referred to mutually desiring normatively gendered males, which Divina did not fit by virtue of her gender-transformative appearance and self-description. Later I asked if she preferred men or women sexually, thinking that if she desired women, the gay self-appellation could make sense (that is, if she thought of herself as a woman who desired other women, her sexuality would be gay). Divina laughed when she heard this question, and responded, 'Honey, I'm just like you. It's all about men.' When I asked if this meant I was a queen, she replied, 'Yes, you're a queen. I'm a queen. Aren't we all the same? … You're just wearing men's clothes.' Other queens also alternated between describing themselves as transgendered, queen, or gay, often introducing various subcategories ranging from *butch queens* (males who wear men's clothing styles and often act masculine in public) to *posh queens* (males who have well-paying jobs and/or money, dress in expensive, trendy men's fashions, and may or may not be effeminate in their mannerisms) to *thugs* (males whose dress styles and mannerisms emulate popular rap and dance-hall singers), who were described by Gigi as just another type of 'C class' queen, meaning that while they were rude, aggressive, and common in their behaviour, they were still, in the end, queens.

This 'code switching' between terms in some Bajan queens' conversations does not necessarily indicate a scenario in which new, 'foreign' terminologies like *gay* and *transgender* have entered local lexicons and are rubbing up against and possibly replacing local distinctive terms like *queen* (see Altman 2001). While I am quite sure that sexual identity terms like *gay* were not created in Bridgetown, many have been in circulation there and throughout Barbados since at least the early to mid-1980s.[5] It is problematic to be still considering such terms foreign when they have been part of the local lexicon for over thirty years and possibly longer. However, instead of framing the argument in terms of local versus foreign sexual terminologies (which carries more than a whiff of the problematic rubric of 'authentic versus corrupted' culture debates), I think it is more productive to foreground the ways in which these socio-sexual and gendered identifications overlap and abut, but never fully collapse into each other, and thus convey, as David Valentine has suggested, alternative ways of thinking through and organizing bodies and their desires (2007). Valentine's ethnographic work among individuals in New York City who are labelled transgender by LGBT (lesbian, gay, bisexual, and transgendered) and queer activists and community support groups revealed that many, but not all, individuals who are working class, Latino, or African American often make claims similar to those of the Bajan queens, that is, 'I've been gay all my life, been a woman all my life' (3). Valentine draws attention to *transgender* as a term 'with a history and a politics' and charts its rise in popularity in the United States, focusing on the way in which it reflects a particular separation and configuration of gender and sexuality that has been developed primarily by and for white, middle-class homosexual men and works to exclude others who do not conform to this division. Valentine argues that these exclusions often operate in terms of race and class where overt (read *performatively effeminate*) homosexuality is not compatible with white middle-class status and employment (43). Therefore, since the 1970s, homosexuality has been defined primarily upon the premise that gender and sexuality exist as two distinct, experiential categories. Male homosexuality has been defined primarily in terms of sexual orientation; in terms of gender, male homosexuals are normative masculine male-bodied individuals who are no different from their heterosexual counterparts except for what they do in the bedroom (61–3). *Gay* has thus come to represent a gender-normative sexual orientation. If an anatomically male individual desires another male but thinks of himself as a woman and dresses like a woman, he is no longer gay but transgender; in essence, his gendered desires trump his sexual ones in terms of placement in this arbitrary dual structure of gender and sexuality.

In his work with African American and Latina sex workers Valentine describes the complex terminological terrain that they employ to describe themselves and others, which at times resonates strongly with the queens' descriptions of themselves and the Bajan scene. Perhaps most important in relation to the Bajan queens' conversations, Valentine asks us to think about what it would mean 'to talk about butch queens, butches, fem queens, women, transsexual women and butch queens up in drags as all, simply, "gay"' (84). In other words, when a male-bodied individual discusses how living and/or performing as a woman does *not* preclude her from being gay (where *gay* indexes erotic desire by and for someone who is male bodied), we should be attempting to make sense of her subjectivity from a position that does not assume that bodies, desires, and identifications can only be understood through conceptually distinct categories of gender and sexuality (see also Kempadoo 2004, 27–8). At the same time, we cannot dismiss completely the Euro-American gender-sexuality framework and its attendant terminologies that are utilized in some of the narratives such as Cherry's.

When some queens like Darcy, Divina, and Didi use *transgender*, *gay*, and *queen* interchangeably for any male-bodied individual who desires another male-bodied individual, they are organizing bodies and their desires in ways that, at the very least, trouble Western mainstream LGBT categories and queer scholarship that are presupposed upon a particular arrangement of distinctions between gender and sexuality: if male-bodied individuals who desire other male-bodied individuals – running the gamut from those who dress and act like women to those who dress and act like heteronormative men – are all labelled gay, then it would seem that sexual object desire operates as the categorical imperative. However, if this same range of individuals also labels themselves *queens*, a term that infers effeminate or feminine behavioural and sartorial characteristics, then it would seem that what we (using a Euro-American framework) call *gender* is operating as the categorical imperative. There is simply no way that gender and sexuality can be completely and separately distinguished in these formulations; yet I am not convinced that we can fully abandon them as analytical frameworks because they do help us to understand how desire, bodies, and behaviours are not reducible to simple dualities constructed through biological determinism (cf. Butler 1990, 1993). At the very least, many of the Bajan queens' fluid terminologies acknowledge the sexual and gendered heterogeneity of their own and others' desires and identities.[6]

This deep entanglement of gender and sexuality in some of the queens' descriptions of themselves and the people they knew may also help to explain the absence of gay-identified individuals in more public contexts like the media, the community, and activist leadership roles. As noted at the beginning of this chapter, Bajan queens are socially visible not only through the obvious fact that by virtue of their dress and comportment they stand out in everyday contexts such as the street, bar, and workplace, but also through the fact that some, such as Didi and Darcy, have been identified as spokespersons for the gay community through their leadership in United *Gays and Lesbians* Against Aids in Barbados (my emphasis), or in media articles where they are asked about gay life in Barbados and/or identified as a gay person. For example, for a two-page article about Didi in the *Nation* the headline read 'Didi the Daring Diva'; to the right of it, in bold text, was a caption reading 'Didi never had any doubt about his sexual orientation: "I knew I was gay from the time I was born,"' which accompanied a photograph of Didi in her Kadooment band costume and another one of him wearing well-tailored pants and a shiny shirt with a colourful scarf wrapped around his neck (Henry and Hall 2004). Another article titled 'The King of Queens' reviewed Divina's and her fellow drag queens' performance at a bar in Holetown, and the journalist wrote that she 'indulged in artistic depravity once again with the three queens of drama' (Lovely 2005, 18). Thus, in public discourses such as the media, queens are the only visible representatives of any gay community or identity, leaving other, more gender-normative homosexual identities unmarked or in some cases marked as underground, down-low, and/or dangerous in terms of their potential threat as carriers of HIV and other sexually transmitted diseases into the heterosexual population. In other words, the public perception of gay is synonymous with that of queen, so that the latter category operates as the default public representation of homosexuality. While this may not be a problem for queens like Didi, Divina, and Darcy, gender-normative male individuals who identify as gay (and do not necessarily identify as queens) may seek to avoid any public disclosure of their identity because they fear being assumed to be effeminate like the queens or they fear being harassed by those who have come to associate gay with disease and duplicity.[7]

Bread and Two Faggots

While the queens' terminologies and descriptions of the sex-scape in Barbados were varied and complex, one theme found in most discussions of self and society was that of respectable behaviour versus common and/or 'bombastic' (aggressively loud and raucous) behaviour. As discussed earlier, when the queens and other Bridgetown residents talked about the past, they would often emphasize how the queens of yesteryear were fierce and earned respect from everyone in their neighbourhood through a combination of reputational and respectable practices. The importance of being respected and of acting in a way that was not perceived to be common or rude continued to occupy a central theme in the queens' narratives of their lives in the present day, but it also operated as another means to divide homosexuals (and sometimes the entire population of Barbados) into different categories. Gigi was particularly articulate on this issue. As I noted earlier, it was Gigi who divided gay people into different categories: A, B, and C class.

GIGI: You call the A class person [someone] who already have it made, have a good income, nice job; they've got a house and are mostly older. And persons in the B class are persons who are on that path, who want to make themselves someone, who are working very hard, working their ass off. They are trying to succeed in life and they don't depend on no one or any person. But C class now is the ones who are just, like, want to drag you down, pull you down. They are commoners. We call them *bread and two faggots*.

DAVID MURRAY: What does that mean, *bread and two faggots*?

GIGI: Fishcakes, you know; we call fishcakes *bread and two*. There is two fishcakes in a salt-bread, yes? So they call them *bread and two*; that is what they're worth.

DAVID: So bread and two faggots is, like, the lowest low?

GIGI: Yeh, the lowest low, $1.50.

DAVID: Wow, that's cheap!

GIGI: Yes, very cheap. (*laughter*)

Not surprisingly, Gigi described herself as a B class on the way to an A class individual. Gigi worked for a small company in Bridgetown, and thus had a regular income. He also worked in the fashion industry and was paid to organize the occasional fashion show for his designer friends. While acknowledging she was not a posh queen (another term for the A class), she clearly admired this group and aspired to be like it.

While other queens were not quite as fine grained in their analysis of queer classes, there were consistent references to other queens or gays whose behaviour was inappropriate and reflected poorly on the community as a whole. Darcy spoke about how she wanted to make her bar look nice so that it would be known as a 'respectable place' where gays and lesbians could enjoy themselves and other people would see that they were not 'low life.' He also noted that the bar attracted men from 'all different levels of society,' from working-class neighbourhoods to the wealthier suburbs in the hills around Bridgetown. When I asked her to elaborate on these different kinds of men, she responded, 'There are different circles of gays here, different levels, but society is a state of mind. You can have a bigger house, car, job, but in the end you come here [the bar] to meet boys.' I interpreted this comment to convey a slightly different position from that of Gigi on stratification among gays and queens in Barbados: whereas Gigi's divisions created the impression of separate and distinct classes that did not interact with each other (especially the A class), Darcy's description acknowledged class distinctions but simultaneously emphasized their temporary transcendence through similar desires, which placed them outside any heteronormative class structure.

Two points emerge from these descriptions of gay and queen classes. First, status, often described in terms of socio-economic difference but also in terms of comportment and interpersonal social skills, is an important structuring principle of difference within queer networks in Barbados, which is not particularly surprising as there is much discussion in research on Barbadian society of the important ways in which class structures and separates – that is, in terms of a small elite white landowner and business class; a now growing Afro-Caribbean middle class of educators, civil servants, and entrepreneurs; and a still significant Afro-Caribbean working class that continues to struggle to make ends meet (Beckles 1990; Barrow and Greene 1979; Freeman 2007). The second point is the importance of respectability and reputation as a dynamic social ethos that simultaneously creates, re-inscribes, and transcends gendered, classed, and sexual divisions in Barbados (Freeman 2007, 5). In the queens' statements we witness tension between their idealized vision of an egalitarian unified community (whether it be among queens, gays, heterosexuals, or all Bajans) premised upon the mutual respect of all fellow citizens, and their perceived reality of a community riven by stress, envy, and resentment owing to gendered, sexual, and socio-economic differences, which therefore requires each individual to be prepared to be fierce and 'look out for herself' or at least distance himself from others who insult, attack, and deride.

Conclusion

I began this chapter by asking whether Bajan sexual diversity or the Bajan sexscape might be organized in ways that partially overlap or are co-constitutive with hegemonic queer Euro-American discourses of identity, community, and activism, but its sexual practices and subjectivities might be refracted through other discursive sociocultural, political, and economic influences generated locally and transnationally. Based on the analysis of the narratives of individuals who identify themselves as gay, queen, transgender, or some combination of these terms, I have argued that while sexual diversity in Barbados is immersed in and partially produced through historical and contemporary Euro-American gendered and sexual politics and identities, it is simultaneously produced in and through a relationship to local gendered and sexual-identity politics, which requires us to acknowledge the ongoing influence of a colonized past and its attendant classed, raced, and cultural dynamics that produce unstable, unpredictable, multiple possibilities of sexual subjectivities. This sex-scape is neither an illustration of a creolized, hybrid culture nor a pluralistic compendium of multiple, discrete cultures. The queens' understandings of themselves, their controversial visibility, and the relative public invisibility of gays and lesbians reflect subjectivities and positionalities that simultaneously challenge and reveal their embeddedness in any singular Western or African, gendered or classed, framework. Certain aspects of their narratives align with working-class queers of colour in the United States and thus suggest parallel experiences as diasporic racialized subjects negotiating white supremacist heteropatriarchal colonization as a frame for identity production. At the very least, they illustrate the ongoing tension between differentially located and produced subjectivities and values, which are pieced together in myriad, contextually shifting ways by individuals who are marginalized by virtue of their non-heteronormative desires and identifications. The result is contextually produced subject positions that may appear to be blended, multiple, or fractured from a Euro-American socio-sexual perspective, but these terms reflect more the social and analytical frameworks of the researcher than they do the viewpoint of the Bajan queens. Indeed, the queens' self-understanding is produced through a local ethos that is influenced by multiple factors, where individual identity is constructed through a complex, fluid calculus of classed, raced, sexed, and gendered roles and values. Key components in the construction and evaluation of many of these roles are the principles of respectability and reputation, which are dynamic and fluid in their meanings as they are located in different communities and social networks.

In their stories of the past and present the queens stressed the importance of having a combination of respectable behaviours and a reputation for talking hard or fighting back if they were challenged or insulted. Related to respectability was status, often described in terms of socio-economic difference but also in terms of comportment and interpersonal social skills, thus operating as a structuring principle of difference within the queer community (and reflecting its importance throughout Barbadian society). Respectability and reputation are therefore a dynamic social ethos that simultaneously create, re-inscribe, and transcend gendered, classed, raced, and sexual divisions in Barbados.

Worth repeating is the cautionary proviso that this chapter represents only a partial glimpse into the complex and rich terrain of sexual diversity in Barbados; gay-identified males, bisexuals, and lesbians were mentioned in my interviews and circulated through media discourses, and thus they merit further investigation for their views on everyday Bajan social life. Chapter 7 provides further insights into the lives of some gay-identified Bajan men, but further research is necessary on the means through which gendered, racial, status, or class divisions may or may not segregate queer people in Barbados, producing different value systems and subjectivities. The next chapter provides some insight into the ways in which local sexual subjectivities are produced in relation to new technologies and regional connections with other Caribbean islands, but further research is still required on the influence of wider diasporic African movements, aesthetics, identifications, and organizations on sexual subject formations.

Finally, we cannot forget the obvious but central fact that the presence of sexual diversity in this society does not equal the celebration of it. It is doubtful that queens have ever had it easy in Barbados; terms like *buller* and *she-she man* have been around for a long time and have been utilized as insults in public contexts, and the queens face daily battles of harassment as they try to go about their business (see Crichlow 2004b). Yet it is equally problematic if we lapse into making overgeneralizing statements like 'Barbados is a homophobic society,' because they silence and flatten out the complex ways in which bodies and their desires are organized and evaluated in everyday life. As researchers and activists we must continue to focus on these rich, diverse everyday narratives, interactions, and performances or we run the risk of creating the very thing that we are trying to challenge.

Chapter 6

Digisex: Cellphones, Barbadian Queens, and Circuits of Desire in the Caribbean

Act I. The Jamaican Invasion

One Sunday in January 2005, Cynthia (whom we met in the previous chapter), Fabric Land, and Steven stopped by my apartment unannounced, 'Just to say hello.' As usual, once we were sitting around the kitchen table, sipping glasses of mauby (a local drink), talk turned to love lives, but this time the conversation went in a very different direction from the usual complaints about 'wutless' (worthless) Barbadian men who could not be trusted and who only exploited the queens. Cynthia informed me that since I had last seen them (about four weeks, prior to returning to Toronto for the Christmas holidays), all three of them had fallen in love with Jamaican men. What was unique about this situation was that only Fabric Land had actually met her man, Cedric, who had visited Barbados with his friend Meesha, a Jamaican drag queen, a couple of months before. Fabric Land and Cedric had been talking and texting 'practically every night' on their cellphones, and Cedric had now linked up Cynthia and Steven with two Jamaican men 'who are real sweet,' according to Cynthia, even though they had not yet met them in person. Cynthia said that she, too, was talking to her man almost every night, and she could tell he was good and faithful and that he would be a perfect husband for her. Steven was also quite sure that he and his man would work out because he had been slowly getting more personal. He said he did not want to give his Jamaican man the wrong impression by asking intimate questions too early on, but he could tell his man was honest and romantic.

Within two weeks all three Jamaicans had arrived in Barbados and moved in with their respective queens. Within four weeks three more Jamaican men had been linked with Bajan queens through cellphone calls and text messages and were soon on their way to Barbados.

This chapter expands on one of the objectives introduced in the previous chapter, that is, to analyse how and why Bajan queens do not mirror Euro-American sexual subjectivities and their relationships to hegemonic socio-sexual values. I now turn to focus on regional or intra-Caribbean circuits of knowledge, desire, and identity in order to explore the ways in which local sexual subjectivities are performed or transformed. I present a short story in three acts about a group of Bajan queens (some of whom have already been introduced in earlier chapters) and their romantic liaisons with Jamaican men. In the analytical sections following each act, I will argue that this small-scale 'drama' (a term used by a number of these queens when describing the events) can tell us something about the way in which intimacy, sexual relationships, and a relatively new form of communications technology – the cellphone – are constituted and interrelated in the Anglo-Caribbean, which in turn speaks to larger issues of same-sex sexual identity and desire, the role and significance of technology, and the complex relationship between globalization, regional relations, and local identities and practices.

I will also engage with arguments about globalization's impact on intimacy and sexuality, in which new communications technologies are often identified as a primary source of cultural transformation and change (Appadurai 1996; Babb 2004; Horst 2006; Padilla et al. 2007). This story of the Bajan queens, their Jamaican boyfriends, and cellphones both underscores and troubles arguments about the transformative potential of technology and the structure and movement of globalizing discourses, economies, and values (Goggin 2007; Horst and Miller 2006; Miller and Slater 2000). Following Collier and Ong's (2005) conceptualization of 'global assemblages,' I will try to demonstrate how these technology-mediated relationships and their associated material, physical, and sentimental exchanges simultaneously reflect and enhance particular Afro-Caribbean ideas about romance, sex, and national difference (Kempadoo 2003, 2004; Puar 2001), which in turn allows me to re-present my argument set forth in the previous chapter through a different lens; that is, I argue that these new technologies, embedded in global capitalist flows, do not necessarily result in an inevitable movement of Western, Northern, developed sexual knowledges, identities, or values to southern, developing peoples and places (Altman 2001; for critiques of Altman see Binnie 2004; Cruz-Malave and Manalansan 2002; Quiroga 2000). Rather, we see how these technologies are adapted to enhance and, to a certain extent, transform *regional* circuits of mobility, pleasure, and desire. These new and rapidly changing circuits of desire thus destabilize the fixed polarities (West and non-West, North and South, or centre and periphery) of cultural models of globalization (Oswin 2006, 779). In this particular case, we see the intensification of a particular Afro-Caribbean circuit of same-sex knowledge, sentiment, and identity, in which ideas about sameness and difference across the Anglo-Caribbean region are created, re-inscribed, and transformed.

Returning to the events noted above, we must first and foremost acknowledge the significance of the cellphone in fostering these new, long-distance romantic relationships. Horst and Miller's ethnographic study of the popularity of the cellphone in Jamaica (2006) provides important background information on the marketing and, more importantly, the local consumptive practices of this piece of technology, which help to explain its central role in the story.[1] Prior to 2001, Jamaica, like Barbados, had only one telephone company, Cable and Wireless plc. However, the Jamaican government's liberalization of the telecommunications industry allowed new companies, like Ireland-based Digicel, to enter the Jamaican market. By 2004 it was estimated that 86 per cent of Jamaicans over the age of fifteen owned a cellphone, and of those who owned a cellphone 70 per cent used the Digicel network (Horst and Miller 2006, 19, 29). Digicel's remarkable success was due in part to an aggressive marketing campaign that, among other things, lowered the cost of international calls by 30 per cent and introduced extremely low-cost texting (sending written messages from cellphone to cellphone) and chat rooms, similar to those on the Internet, that allowed subscribers to join particular themed 'rooms' in which text messages could be sent and received (Horst and Miller 2006, 25, 87, 72). In Barbados the statistics were similar: in 2006 there was close to one cellphone per person (Caribbean Telecommunications Union 2007), and even though Digicel entered the cellphone market later (in 2004) than did Cable and Wireless, it quickly grew to rival the powerful company in popularity (Digicel, personal communication 2008).

However, as Horst and Miller note, the popularity of the cellphone cannot be explained in terms of good marketing strategies alone. In other words, we must look into the ways in which cellphones enhance existing modes of connectivity and historically established desires. Horst and Miller focus on the working poor of Jamaica, where they observe how the cellphone contributes to the maintenance of a variety of often overlapping social networks (kin, friends, lovers, business associates) through the concept of the 'link-up,' in which regular, often short-length calls or texts are made to keep in contact with one's social networks (2006, 89). Cellphone users also appreciate the phone's ability to allow them to manage their social affairs better by not restricting them to a particular place when they need to make or receive a call and by allowing more privacy through the phone's portability and its texting functions (Horst and Miller 2006).

The daily conversations and text-message exchanges between Bajan queens and their Jamaican boyfriends most likely could not have existed prior to the arrival of Digicel in the Caribbean region, which has made inter-island communication more affordable through lower long-distance rates and texting. Most of the queens involved in these relationships were from working-class neighbourhoods in Bridgetown, were employed in full- or part-time work (ranging from gas-station cashiers to retail sales, hairdressing, dressmaking, or sex work), and told me that they were proud to be 'independent,' but their earnings often barely covered the costs of basic necessities like rent, food, and transportation. However, everyone owned a cellphone and justified its use to me in terms that echoed Horst and Miller's findings with Jamaicans. Additionally, some queens mentioned that they felt more secure with their cellphone; Fabric Land said that if she was walking down a street and felt unsafe, she could call up one of her sisters and know that they would be there to 'have my back' in a few minutes.

It is important, however, to re-emphasize Horst and Miller's point that this particular telecommunications technology *enhances*, rather than invents or creates, social practices and values (2006, 5), when one considers its significance in initiating these romantic liaisons. Remember that the initial contact between these two groups was through the visit of a drag queen and her friend from Jamaica. Regional migration and recreational travel is a long-standing feature of Caribbean societies: the working poor often seek employment in prosperous islands near and far; people make visits to family members who are working and living on other islands; both the working class and the middle class vacation on other islands (Gmelch and Gmelch 1997, 178). Of the eight queens that I knew well, seven had been off the island at some point (ranging from a brief trip to see family in nearby Grenada to years of living and working in the United States), although I was told by Cynthia that quite a few of the ones 'working the street' had never travelled abroad. Thus initial contact between the Jamaicans and Bajans was made via a long-standing tradition of inter-Caribbean travel and was then enhanced or intensified through the presence of cellphones, which allowed for daily talk and texting across great distances that were previously prohibitively costly, resulting in the queens' belief that they were in love with these men because they had come to know them through intimate talk.

We might also note at this point that the queens' discourse of romantic love emerged at a very early stage of the relationships (prior to any face-to-face or physical contact), rendering it distinct from dominant Western gay discourses of romance. Whereas, in most popular Western gay narratives, sexual compatibility is identified as the primary and often most critical component in determining whether or not two men will be romantically compatible, the queens assured me that they knew they were in love through their phone conversations with their Jamaican mates. Steven said that he had been asking his man 'personal' questions, which led him to believe that his man would be 'faithful' and 'honest,' qualities that the other queens often repeated in their descriptions of what they found appealing in their men, and which differentiated the latter from Barbadian men who 'lie, cheat, and steal,' according to Fabric Land.

These queens' descriptions of perfect and imperfect male partners resonate with the gendered romantic ideals and tensions circulating through heterosexual, Afro-Caribbean popular culture. In her study of the ways in which the cellphone has been incorporated into performances of sex and sexuality in Jamaica, Tanya Batson Savage notes that women and men in her study felt that the cellphone both aided and thwarted intimacy (2007). While both sexes enjoyed and appreciated the ways in which they could create and intensify their intimacy with each other (through more regular contact and romantic and sexually explicit text messages), they also noted that the cellphone could be used by the men to maintain multiple relationships and therefore allowed them to be more deceitful (Batson Savage 2007). This latter characteristic of men re-inscribes a long-established popular trope of masculinity in the Afro-Caribbean (Chevannes 2001; Kempadoo 2003), although it should be noted that the Bajan queens made a distinction between trustworthy Jamaican and untrustworthy Bajan men at this point in their relationships, thus potentially troubling these pan-Afro-Caribbean tropes of gendered identity and difference. We will see below how this theory of differentiated national masculinities held up after a few months.

Act II. Jamaica as Gay Central? The Formation of Regional Sexual Knowledges

Over the next few weeks there were numerous gatherings at Fabric Land and Steven's apartment, Cynthia's small chattel home,[2] and my apartment. The mood was mostly festive, with lots of sly banter among the queens about their own and their friends' relationships, noting that, for example, Ryan and Leroy had no time for anyone but themselves and that they could hear wedding bells off in the distance. There was also much comparative talk about gay life in Barbados and in Jamaica. The Bajan queens (and I) were interested in what the Jamaicans had heard about Barbados prior to arriving here. Cedric said that it was a destination many of his gay friends wanted to visit as they had heard that Barbados had a reputation for being an island 'full a *chi chi man*' (a Jamaican term for 'homosexuals') and that gay life here was supposed to be more open and 'tolerable.' However, in the few weeks that Cedric had been here he decided that this was an erroneous stereotype and that in fact Barbados's gay life was dull and boring. Jayson also felt that 'Jamaicans will leave you alone more than Bajans; they don't gossip and stir up as much.' The queens and I found this hard to believe, but over the next few days when I asked the other visiting Jamaicans to make the same comparison, they all agreed with Cedric's and Jayson's assessments. First of all, Jayson said not to believe all the reports published by the human rights organizations that state that gay Jamaicans are always threatened with violence and death. In fact, 'the life' there was much more lively than in Barbados, and there were very few problems as long as you did not 'push it in other people's faces.' Jayson said that as long as you 'managed yourself' by not being overly 'showy,' you would be okay. He then got up and imitated a swishy walk (which to me resembled a female model on a fashion runway), saying this would attract trouble. Cedric said that he was very private in his neighbourhood and made sure that people who came over did not arouse suspicion. There was no problem with having men over most of the time, he said, as neighbours thought they were just friends. Jayson and Cedric lived in Montego Bay, which they said was very cool with gay people, and at the clubs they all mixed, no problem. Cedric went on to say that it was easy to pick up men in Jamaica, and it was getting easier. He then stood up and announced that in five years homosexuality would be decriminalized. How could he say this? he asked rhetorically. 'First of all,' he went on, 'the straight boys are now wearing the gay boys' outfits – they wear tight pants and shirts, which show off everything. There's less and less difference between straights and gays, and the old codes (earring in one ear, ring on a thumb) don't mean a thing anymore.' Byron, another Jamaican, added that it was easy to talk about men in public ; he and his friend used code words to refer to hot guys, like 'She is fab' (meaning 'He is hot'), 'Look at she big breast' ('Look at his big dick'), or 'She ah one o dem' ('He's one of them,' to confirm he is gay). 'Furthermore,' Cedric continued, 'there are more men coming up and introducing themselves to me and my friends' or stating their interest in public. There were also more men in South Kingston who were willing to have sex with men for money. 'No problem to get someone to suck your dick if you offer a few bucks,' added one of the other Jamaicans. Jayson said that there were often guys who insulted him and were nasty when they were with their friends on the streets, but at night they came looking.

The Jamaicans agreed that cellphones had made a difference. As Jayson said, 'one of the main ways that guys are connecting with other guys in Jamaica now is through Digicel's text messaging chat rooms, where you can post messages, exchange phone numbers and other information. This is the main way to learn about where parties are, if someone's been hurt, and of course to meet other men.' Jayson continued by saying that when their cellphones ring, they say,

'It's Digisex calling.' 'With Digisex, you could easily find a party to attend every weekend, and often there were multiple events happening on the same night.' The Bajan queens were notably impressed by this and hoped that Digicel would soon offer the same service in Barbados. As final proof of their argument, Jayson went into his room and returned with a gay calendar produced in Jamaica, which, Cedric said, was hung in many offices and restaurants.

While I often wanted to question the rationale through which the Jamaicans evaluated their society as more gay positive (that is, the fact that managing oneself in public seemed to me to be more about learning how to perform heteronormative masculinity in a way that would not draw attention to one's same-sex sexual desires), more significant was the fact that the Bajan queens did not challenge or dispute the Jamaicans' evaluation of gay life in Barbados, and by the end of some of these conversations some said that they were going to start planning a trip to Jamaica. However, I think the appeal of Jamaica, as represented through these men's presentations, was as much due to the ways in which it resonated similarity as much as difference to the Bajan queens, in that they could identify with the contours of gendered and sexual performativity and practice in Jamaica. When, in other interviews with queens and self-identified gay Bajans, I would ask them to describe the scene in Barbados, the portrait would be similar, at least in terms of emphasizing the importance of managing one's gendered performances in public spaces. This was especially the case for queens who described themselves to me as 'real women' because they lived their everyday lives dressing, acting, and looking like women (as opposed to butch queens who would masquerade as men by wearing men's clothes when they were in public or at work but would go in drag to the local bar or private parties) and, in doing so, would attract negative attention; comments, taunts, and ridicule were part of any expedition through public spaces like downtown streets, stores, or government offices. However, it was not just the effeminate queens explicitly challenging masculine performances in public who risked ridicule. Omar, who self-identified as gay but was 'undercover' (his term for signalling that he was not out about his sexuality) at work and home, would often comment on my inappropriate clothing choices, saying that he was embarrassed to be seen with me wearing such tight shirts and short shorts; this totally surprised me, because in my opinion I was wearing conservative-looking clothing according to mainstream gay (white middle-class) cultural norms (that is, what I would term a loose-fitting cotton T-shirt and baggy shorts that ended just above my knees).[3] Thus, whether one identified as a queen or a gay male, the management of gendered performativity, particularly in relation to the perception of effeminacy, occupied a central role in the construction of a socio-sexual identity in Barbados. I would argue that as they listened to their boyfriends' stories of life in Jamaica, the Bajans were attracted to a Jamaican gendered sex-scape that was similar to their own – that is, a network of men that was raced, gendered, and sexed through similarly coded performances that operate just beneath or within everyday spaces of gendered heteronormativity, except that in Jamaica the network of same-sex connections appeared to be more frequent and accessible thanks to telecommunications technologies like Digicel's chat rooms and the larger scale of Jamaican society in general (that is, its larger geographic size and population, which appeared to provide more choices and relative anonymity).

However, while the question of whether Barbados's and Jamaica's gendered and sexual performances are similar or different (and why) is interesting and merits further research, I think it is equally important to draw attention to the way in which these conversations between Bajans and Jamaicans were productive in forming and exchanging knowledge about sexual and gendered identities and practices in everyday life across the Caribbean. Furthermore, when we keep in mind the way these conversations came to pass in the first place – through the movement and circulation of Afro-Caribbean subjects and the communication between them, and through their use of the particular technologies that were made available through neoliberal global economic policies that emphasized 'free' trade and 'open' competitive markets (albeit with the profits of these markets returning to European corporate headquarters of multinational corporations like Digicel) – we begin to see more clearly the complexities of globalization and its effects on local values and practices of sexuality, desire, and intimacy.

Anthropologists have increasingly noted problems in theories of globalization, including, first, the fact that these so-called new flows of capital, labour, and ideas across vast spaces are deeply embedded in histories of similar movements, a point that is particularly applicable to the Caribbean. Second, the assumption that there is a unidirectional flow of capital, ideas, and policies from wealthy developed nation states of the West or North to undeveloped or underdeveloped nations and peoples of the South is highly contestable; the landscape of political and economic power is uneven and always changing, such that new centres of power are emerging as others decline, which challenges any model presupposed upon a fixed geopolitical framework for the organization and movement of power. Third, the assumption that the end result of globalization is the gradual homogenization of culture in the mould of Western liberal democratic capitalism is also highly questionable (Thomas and Clarke 2006). As I noted in the introduction to this book, in the field of sexuality studies a similar discussion has emerged around the problem of trans-local sexual politics, identities, and practices, where once again some anthropologists raised red flags when claims of the emergence of a universal, 'global gay' identity (Altman 2001) were made. While it is important to acknowledge the increased visibility and circulation of a particular formation of gay identity and desire that is racially, politically, and economically structured through Euro-American, liberal-democratic, and political-economic frameworks, the ways in which this particular formation is strategically adapted, fused, transformed, or mutated in various local contexts renders any reductionist or essentialist identity paradigm deeply problematic (see Binnie 2004; Boellstorff 2007; Cruz-Malave and Manalansan 2002; Manalansan 2003; Oswin 2006). However, as Padilla et al. (2007) have noted, there continues to be a lack of ethnographic research identifying the appearance of local productions, displays, and practices of desire and intimacy in a globalizing context: what are their operations, their discursive material, or their ideological effects? What are the microsociological interpersonal and emotional responses of individual actors to the broad changes that are occurring as a consequence of globalization? I would add to this the challenge of identifying global processes in terms of heterogeneous, contingent, partial, and situational assemblages, which link individuals and groups into networks that traverse multiple geographic spaces or locations (Collier and Ong 2005). In other words, these global assemblages are not organized simply or only in terms of the movement of a global discourse or object into a local space, culture, or identity; rather, they circulate in obtuse, refractory, non-linear networks that may be organized through parallel similarities or complementarities based on race, class, history, sexuality, and/or regional proximity. While I am in no way denying the hegemony of a global political-economic and cultural marketplace, I am trying to draw attention to the ways in which we can think about alternative or multiple globalizations occurring through parallel tropes or continuums other than, or in addition to, the 'modern West versus the rest.'

Thus, in the narratives of Jamaican versus Bajan gay life presented above, while not denying that a hegemonic Euro-American model of gay sexual identity may have influenced the Jamaicans' and Barbadians' sexual subjectivities and that particular forms of global capitalism have precipitated the presence and use of new communication technologies and thus new kinds of relationships, I am arguing that it is equally important to think about how Anglo-Afro-Caribbean sexual knowledges are being created and circulated through these conversations. I think it is notable that in these conversations there was no explicit reference to any North American or European gay community, culture, or identity. The primary comparative context through which understandings of socio-sexual life were articulated was intra-Caribbean. The Jamaicans maintained that gay life was better in Jamaica, thus asserting difference between two Caribbean nation states, although, as I have argued, their descriptions of socio-sexual life, gendered performativity, and engagement with everyday heteronormativity were similar to the descriptions I heard from Bajans about life in Barbados. We might therefore be tempted to think of these conversations as snapshots of diaspora in the making because they do not fit easily into a discrete sexual (gay), racial/ethnic (black/Afro), or class (working -poor) model of diasporic identity; elements of all three coexist simultaneously in these conversations.

Act III. The Jamaica-Barbados Accord Unravels

By the end of February the Jamaican-Barbadian relationships were fraying. Cedric and Fabric Land had a big fight on the street in front of Darrel's Bar, a local rum shop frequented by queens and gay men in a central Bridgetown neighbourhood. I was not there that night, but the next morning I received a call from Cedric on his cellphone, informing me that they had not been speaking to each other all week; Cedric was tired of Fabric Land's 'drama,' that is, turning everything into an argument (Fabric Land later informed me that she was tired of Cedric asking her for money all the time when she did not have any). The breaking point came when Fabric Land saw Cedric talking to a good-looking guy at Darrel's Bar, went up to them, and pushed the guy away from Cedric, saying, 'Stay away from my man.' Cedric was furious and started to yell at Fabric Land, saying he had a right to talk to whomever he wanted. Fabric Land accused him of flirting with numerous men and other queens since he had arrived in Barbados and said that she was not going to put up with it any longer. This led to, as Fabric Land put it, a *bassa-bassa* (Bajan dialect for 'fight' or 'quarrel') on the street. Cedric was now sleeping in the living room of another queen who was paired with a Jamaican. He wanted to leave Barbados but did not have the funds available to pay for changing his ticket.

Meanwhile Jayson was becoming stressed out by all the malicious gossip. He told me that, when he and Byron (another Jamaican) had walked into town together a few times, people had called Cynthia (Jayson's mate) on their cellphones, saying they had just seen Jayson together with another queen and wondering whether Cynthia knew about this. Even though Cynthia knew who Byron was and said that she believed Jayson when he assured her that they were just friends, Jayson felt that he was now under constant surveillance and that Cynthia became suspicious whenever he left the house without her; she would call him constantly on his cellphone to ask what he was doing, who he was with, and when he was returning home. Jayson said that he was purposely letting the credit on his phone run out so that he would have an excuse for not answering it. Furthermore, he said that Cynthia had started to complain about how much money he asked her for, which he felt was unfair because she knew that he was not working in Jamaica when she invited him to Barbados, and she had assured him that she would look after everything and he would have nothing to worry about.

One night, while I was driving Latesha home from her weekly drag show at a west coast hotel, she mentioned to me that Cedric had been hitting on her constantly since he had arrived in Barbados and had been calling her from his cellphone every day, but she was not interested in him or any of the Jamaicans. She believed that most of the Jamaicans came to the island because they knew that the queens were well off financially and therefore they could live off them. Latesha said that she was proud of what she had accomplished and of her financial independence. She lived in a very new-looking flat in Bridgetown with another queen and was working as a manager at one of the call centres in Bridgetown in addition to doing the evening drag shows. She could easily find Cedric a job, she went on, but she did not trust him and would wait until she found a 'real' man who could support her.

I did not know whom or what to believe anymore. The queens had a fairly consistent way of presenting their lives: in their narratives it was usually others who initiated courtship, and they almost always seemed to be the 'innocent' recipients of this attention. They would tell me that they were looking for men who were pure of intention, but they knew that many would use them for financial support and would leave them when they found a 'real' woman. Furthermore, there was envy and jealousy among the queens, I was often reminded. As one queen said, they are each other's best friends and worst enemies and have the least trust in each other when it comes to gossiping about their men.

By early March the Jamaican situation had become enough of an issue that it was raised at a monthly meeting of UGLAAB. Most of the members of the group in attendance that night (twelve including me) were from working-class neighbourhoods in and around Bridgetown, so it was not too surprising that there was knowledge of the Jamaicans' presence. Towards the end of this meeting a member asked if the group should be concerned with this 'Jamaican invasion' because some felt that the Jamaicans were exploiting the queens, and furthermore their health status was unknown. Another member said that he had heard rumours that the queens had flown the Jamaicans over; another member disagreed, saying that he knew the queens and that this was untrue. 'In fact,' he said, 'some of the Jamaicans are now working here,' but most members nodded their heads in agreement that the queens had a reputation for paying for their men.

By the end of March, about three months after the arrival of the first group of Jamaican boyfriends, Cedric and three other Jamaicans had left Barbados. Jayson was still at Cynthia's house, but he assured me that he would never return to Barbados. 'Too vicious,' he said. One other couple was still together and remained so when I returned to Toronto a few months later.

Once again, the cellphone remains a central character in this final act of the Jamaican-Bajan drama, but its role and significance has changed from that of a technology that aids and abets desire and intimacy to one of a technology that threatens and thwarts them. The cellphone was now a surveillance instrument, the primary means through which information about the movements and actions of the Jamaicans and queens was communicated, often instantly, for example when Cynthia received phone calls from acquaintances who just moments before had spotted her man, Jayson, with another queen on a Bridgetown street. Jayson's decision not to buy more credit for his phone in order not to have to answer Cynthia's constant surveillance calls also illustrates the cellphone's negatively perceived presence. These patterns of practice and negative evaluations of the cellphone resonate once again with Horst and Miller's arguments pertaining to the dialectical relationships between new forms of technology and sociocultural practice and change. Previously I noted that the cellphone had become significant and valued for the ways in which it contributed to creating and maintaining link-ups between the Jamaicans and the Bajans, echoing Horst and Miller's observations on its use and value in working-class communities in Jamaica. Similarly, these negative evaluations of the cellphone resonate closely with Horst and Miller's findings: many of their Jamaican informants felt that cellphones enhanced an atmosphere of suspicion and distrust that already existed in many heterosexual relationships, where a presumption of deceit is pervasive. Owing to its mobility, the cellphone made it easier to lie, inasmuch as the call recipient's location could not be easily traced (which was not the case when only land-line phone calls were available) and the caller was able to make calls or text messages from any location (that is, outside of his or her partner's home or in spaces where no familiar ears might overhear the conversation) (Horst and Miller 2006). Batson Savage's (2007) examination of the relationship between cellphones and heterosexuality in Jamaican popular culture makes a similar argument about its ambiguous position: it both promotes and distils intimacy, in that as much as it is a tool for creating or intensifying intimacy, it can also be a tool for maintaining multiple relationships or revealing duplicity.[4]

Generally, we might observe that the struggles and tensions in these queens' romantic and sexual liaisons mirrored certain qualities of heterosexual relationships in the Afro-Caribbean that have been found in studies of the region (Barrow 1996; Chevannes 2001; Dann 1987; Kempadoo 2004). Not only did they seem to face similar challenges around the issues of honesty and of suspicion of a partner having outside sexual liaisons, which were exacerbated by the presence of the cellphone, but they also manifested generally the tensions between the value of respectability, the importance of material and economic support, and the ideal of romantic love. In Carla Freeman's analysis of discourses of marriage amongst middle-class heterosexual Barbadian entrepreneurs, she notes that their relations follow a general Afro-Caribbean pattern in which marriage and the nuclear family continue to be idealized concepts or aspirations of respectability, but in practice there are a range of union formations in Barbados in which matrifocal households predominate and marriage continues to be an option only exercised by a few (23 per cent of the adult population were married, according to the 2000 Barbados census) (Freeman 2007, 7–8).[5] In the working-class neighbourhoods where most of the queens involved in these relationships lived, most households appeared to follow a similar pattern. While the queens' desired ideal in romantic and sexual relationships mirrored a gendered women's perspective on relationships (that is, the search for 'true love,' emphasizing a search for a faithful, honest male mate with whom they could establish a long-term secure and emotionally intimate relationship), their reputation for economically supporting their male mates disrupted the popular male perception of a woman's objective in a heterosexual relationship (material and financial gain from their male mates), owing to their economic power over their male partners. This economic independence (relatively speaking, in relation to male peers) has long been noted as a feature of working-class Afro-Caribbean women (Barrow 1988; Freeman 2007; Mintz 1989; Reddock 1994), but in these queens' narratives it appears to produce an ambiguous outcome because the queens began to complain of having to support their Jamaican boyfriends, most of whom were unemployed or not able to work in Barbados. Latesha's narrative embodied these tensions as she told me that she was proud to be economically independent and was not going to start a relationship with any of the Jamaicans who were not working. However, her desired mate was one who could support her, indicating a romantic ideal in which she, self-positioned as the woman in the relationship, would no longer have to work and could be financially and materially dependent on her man.

Contrary to much of the analysis of working-class Afro-Caribbean relationships, which dismisses romantic love as subordinate to material needs and economic survival, I would argue that individualized Western romance discourses are significant in the queens' beliefs (at least in the initial stages) about relationships, but these ideals are supplemented, supplanted, and challenged by the pragmatics of the economic and material circumstances in which the queen begins to occupy a role that she perceives as masculine, which in turn troubles the relationship. Trouble also comes in the form of suspicion and gossip about male partners cheating and lying, traits that are often explained as 'natural' components of masculinity (Chevannes 2001). In sum, love and sex were constituted by the queens in ways that both re-inscribed and complicated tropes of heterosexual gendered relations in the Afro-Caribbean.

Conclusion

We see in the last act of this drama an undermining of the theory of distinct national masculinities that the queens presented to me at the outset of their contact with the Jamaicans when they noted that the latter appeared to be more honest, faithful, and romantic than their Bajan counterparts, and yet three months later they were described as just as 'wuthless' and troublesome. Thus the experiences of this group of marginalized sexual subjects, mediated through new communication technologies, relative mobility, and relative economic stability (the queens'), produced knowledges about sex, gender, and society that simultaneously enhanced and transformed existing circuits of desire, sexuality, and identity in the Afro-Caribbean. One transformation occurred in the sense that both of these groups – the Jamaican men and the Bajan queens – in most cases had not known or met their romantic counterparts in person prior to these relationships, but through their experiences with each other they learned something new about themselves and each other's society. At the same time, we might argue that this experience enhanced or re-inscribed the practices and knowledge about gender, sexuality, and society that were already circulating throughout the Anglo-Caribbean; each group certainly knew about the other's society and had perceptions of its culture and people that they initially believed to be distinct, but by the end of their relationships they had re-inscribed familiar tropes of gendered and sexual normativity in the sense that the Bajan queens now perceived the Jamaicans to be no different from the Bajan men in terms of their unfaithful behaviour and financial mooching.[6]

A transformation could also be found in the ways in which intimacy and romance were created, maintained, and broken through technology. Cellphones, and in particular Digicel's aggressively competitive marketing strategies across the Anglo-Caribbean, lowered the cost of long-distance communication and provided these couples with previously unaffordable and unavailable means (that is, texting) of maintaining regular, intimate contact. However, the cellphone was also viewed as a device that could be used to undermine relationships in ways that were not previously possible through its portability and technological capacities (for example, address lists and storage of previously dialled numbers that could be used to discover a partner's lies and deceitful behaviour). At the same time, this inter-island intimacy and its attendant tensions were not entirely new. Movement of Caribbean people across the region, whether in search of work, romance, or play, is a long-established practice, and so too, accordingly, is knowledge of other island societies and their social practices. The cellphone thus facilitated and enhanced certain possibilities between these groups who do not enjoy ease of communication, sociality, and a sentiment of community because of their marginality in their respective societies, but it would be problematic to claim that a singular technology created new social communities, practices, or identities.

Generally, I think we can argue that both parties came away from this experience with their knowledge of their own gendered and sexual behaviours and identities both challenged and re-inscribed, a point that complicates theories of globalization and its effects on local practices, subjectivities, and identities. This story of romance and its entanglements reveals the influence of global capital and communication technologies in a particular region, but it also reveals how these political, material, and economic influences are mediated through other, already existing flows or circuits of knowledge and desire. These circuits do not move in a simple North–South direction but rather circulate throughout and across a particular region long immersed in global flows, whose people share aspects of a colonial past and a political-economic present. At the same time, these regional flows are partially formed and articulated through hegemonic political and economic forces. The story of the Bajan queens and their Jamaican men illustrates the way in which these technology-mediated engagements reveal the interconnectedness of the local, regional, and global and are simultaneously transformative and re-inscriptive in their effects on everyday productions of desire, romance, and knowledge of the sexual self.

Chapter 7

Life Stories

My objective in this chapter is to provide insight into the lives of a few gay-identified men in Barbados through their life stories that were presented to me over the course of two or three one-hour interviews. The interviews focused on the ways in which these men negotiated their sexual desires and public knowledge about gay or homosexual identities at various stages of their lives and viewed homosexuality in Bajan social life past and present. In these narratives we see some opinions and perspectives overlapping with those of the queens presented in the previous chapters, but in other domains there are significantly different positions. However, more important is the fact that the three detailed life stories I present do not demonstrate a singular, identical definition or position on sexuality and gender and their organization and operations in daily Bajan life, although overlapping themes of respectability, properly performed masculinity, and distrust of and/or frustration with other gays or queens appear across the narratives.

These life stories were selected from formal taped interviews with nine self-identified gay men in Barbados.[1] All names, some place names, and other details have been changed in order to ensure anonymity. The three interviewees were Afro-Barbadians who came from poor and/or working-class families (although one, Michael, had clearly moved into a middle-class position through his education and career). This similarity in socio-economic backgrounds is likely due to the fact that most of my initial contacts in Barbados had been made through Joyce and the UGLAAB community, many of whom, as I have discussed in previous chapters, live in poor and/or working-class neighbourhoods in Bridgetown. I also met some of these men through Edward, the bed-and-breakfast owner, who claimed that he had met most of his Barbadian gay friends online or at the tourist bars. I have chosen these three individuals as each represents a different decade in age (Omar was in his twenties, Michael was in his thirties, and Tony was in his forties at the time of the interviews), which allows for the possibility of different perspectives and opinions based on age and generation.[2]

Omar

I met Omar through Edward, the bed-and-breakfast owner. Omar was born 'in the countryside' in 1981 (making him twenty-one years old at the time of our first meeting). He grew up with his grandmother, four sisters, and two brothers (his mother left to work in the United States when he was a child, and was still there, regularly sending home money and goods). Omar remembered his home community as a 'brother-sister neighbourhood, where you could come and pull your door open at any time, and get a share of food ... Everybody knew everybody.' He did not remember knowing or hearing about any gay people or queens, which he thought was due to the fact that the community was so small that if anyone had been like that, they would have to keep it 'on the down-low.' Omar said that he started to think about men sexually when he was sixteen, in fourth form at school. Although he was interested in a couple of boys, he did not pursue them, because 'I am the sort of person that likes to keep my business hush-hush and to myself.' Omar remembered one boy in his class who was teased because 'he was more feminine and flamboyant with the whole hand thing and the whole broadness.' Omar kept his distance from the boy as he did not want anyone to make assumptions about him.

After finishing secondary school, Omar moved to live with his father outside of Bridgetown. His father had two small chattel homes on his property and let Omar live in one, giving him the privacy he desired. Other relatives, including uncles, aunts, and cousins, lived nearby. He began working in the storage facility of a nearby store and gradually moved up to the position of team leader of the storage facility's staff. Omar said that he had never spoken to anyone at work about his sexuality as 'it might become kinda difficult working in that environment with the staff, and the respect that I had worked to build up there would actually go through the door and it would be like, oh, he's a bulla, a *she-she* man, and you can only take so much of that ... so I try to live my life on the DL [down-low].' At the same time, Omar said that it did not really bother him if people talked about him, because 'I am what I am, and there is a certain amount of respect that I demand from everyone regardless of if I am gay or straight.' Omar's first sexual experience occurred through his workplace. He was eighteen years old, working at a store in Bridgetown, and a co-worker noticed that an outside merchandiser who often helped pack the shelves was staring constantly at Omar. Omar gradually realized that this was true, so he went up to the merchandiser and asked if there was something he would like; he responded, 'Yes,' and gave Omar his phone number. After talking a few times on the phone, they met up at the house of the man's relative, which was empty for that night, and eventually started kissing, and Omar realized he really liked this. It did not last long, because it was very difficult for them to meet, and often the only place they could have sex was in the man's car in a parking lot by one of the beaches at night. However, Omar started to meet other gay guys through this man and became friends with some of them.

Omar had not discussed his sexual preference with anyone in his family although he assumed they knew or had figured it out. One of his female cousins once asked him if he could find out whether or not a man in whom she was interested was gay, indicating to him that she assumed he was gay and was okay with it. Another time, his uncle, who lived in a house near Omar's, told Omar's father that there were a lot of men coming and going from his house, but his father 'didn't really pressure me on it.' Nevertheless, a few months after telling me this, Omar had a major falling out with his father over this very issue and told me that he was not going to be able to invite me or any of his friends over to watch movies or hang out.

Omar's family attended a Pentecostal church. Soon after we first met, I asked Omar if he remembered hearing any lectures on homosexuality from the pulpit when he was growing up, but he did not. I told him that from what I had read, most Pentecostal and Evangelical churches were homophobic and would try to 'cure' homosexuals of their 'affliction' or 'sin.' Omar thought that this was ridiculous. He believed that being gay was 'your mentality' and that even if you tried to be straight, 'there would always be that feeling that you want to be intimate with the same sex.' As a religious sceptic, I was not ready to let this topic go; I argued that even if its rationale were faulty, the church could still cause great suffering by making parents and relatives think that their gay son was sick or a sinner. Omar replied, 'Yeh, well, the church will always be the church, and therefore it will stay on in the background ... but at the end of the day, if my child has decided that he is going to be gay, in my religion it might be wrong, but there is nothing saying that I cannot support that he is gay and at least encourage him that if he is going to live the lifestyle, to live it carefully, honestly, and decently. There is nothing in the Bible that states that.' However, over the course of the next three years Omar's position on the church and homosexuality changed.

In an interview in December 2004, Omar and I once again returned to the topic of religion when Omar told me that he had switched from his family's church to a Seventh-day Adventist church down the road from his home because he enjoyed their services and had found a group of people his age with whom he enjoyed liming (hanging out and chatting with friends). Once again, I said that churches like this one were known to be unsupportive of homosexuality, but this time Omar responded differently: 'If they are saying homosexuality is wrong, and the Bible says from the days of Sodom and Gomorrah that it is wrong, I can't go against that … I will not go against that as that is the word of God … but I can say to you that I determine the decision that I make, not you … I listen when they talk about homosexuality and how it is wrong … I grasp the aspects of where they're coming from and the Bible's status, and I don't disagree, because from my faith and religion it's written in the Bible.' When I asked Omar if he felt that what he desired was therefore wrong, he said he questioned it now and sometimes wondered how something 'they say is so wrong can feel so right.' He noted that there were other sections of the Bible that said we were all capable of faults and that we must remember to 'forgive thy neighbour.' He reminded me that Sodom and Gomorrah were not destroyed just because of homosexuality: 'There are many other sinful activities as well. There's no possible way that you could live the whole Bible all the time.' Omar's conflicted position continued in our subsequent conversations, and because I did not do a very good job of keeping my opinion about the church to myself, there was an increased amount of tension around this topic every time it was broached; therefore we both ended up avoiding it. However, it was clear that moving to the Seventh-day Adventist Church had affected Omar's understanding of himself as a homosexual.

Omar had been involved in 'three or four serious relationships,' which had all ended because of the same problem: 'They just want to be controlling and dictating, you know?' It turned out that all of the relationships had been with men who were significantly older (ten years or more) than Omar, and he acknowledged that he had focused on older guys after having had a couple of experiences with men his age that were not satisfactory because the men were so insecure and secretive. Omar's longest relationship was with C., who described himself as bisexual but, a few months after dating Omar, claimed that he was totally in love. C. and Omar were together for two years, although much of the last year was on and off because of numerous fights. While the sex was always great ('he brought out the wild side in me!'), C. was not comfortable going out in public with Omar, nor did he like attending gay events or bars that were known to be frequented by gays, because he was from a higher class (he had an administrative position at a hotel at that time) and did not want people to see him at those places. For a while Omar was willing to do as C. wanted: 'I actually did all that for love, which is why people would say you would do anything for love, which I have proven is true. I had stopped speaking to a lot of my friends, I had stopped going out with them; it was just me going from home to work, from work to church, and from church to up by him. I had isolated myself in his little world.'

In the end, Omar felt he had sacrificed his independence for C. and that he was too young to be 'suffocated' like this. He also felt that C. did not respect the fact that he had a difficult job, where he was on his feet all day, dealing with 'quarrelsome' staff and customers, which often left him exhausted, whereas C. had a comfortable office job and would come home wanting Omar to make dinner and have sex every night. These arguments led to a number of break-ups and make-ups; at one point Omar tried to make C. into 'just a fuck buddy,' but C. was too possessive and jealous. Omar also became worried about contracting HIV/AIDS because C. sometimes tried to have sex with him without a condom, and he knew that C. slept with other people. He once let C. do this and afterwards became so panicked that he fainted at work. A few weeks afterwards he went to the Queen Elizabeth Hospital to get a test. When the doctor asked if he was gay, he said no. (He now realizes that that was the wrong decision as she might have been able to offer him some good advice.) When the test came back negative, Omar decided to always use condoms, but C. 'freaked, saying you shouldn't be walking around with condoms if you and I are together,' so Omar knew that he had to end the relationship. A couple of other relationships followed similar trajectories (in terms of Omar feeling suffocated and distrustful), leading him to contemplate that he might switch over to women. When I pointed out to Omar that this sentiment contradicted his earlier opinion of what I assumed to be an 'innate' gay mentality, he responded that if he wanted to change, he could.

Omar was also frustrated with the fact that (according to him) most Bajan guys were like C. in that they always hid their homosexual desires behind a heterosexual facade. He felt that this was especially the case with those who spent their days acting like 'bad boys,' that is, cussing and dressing 'thug style,' but at night you would see the femininity come out. As I expressed some incredulity at this, Omar elaborated: 'You have to remember, it is all an image for the friends and for society because they cannot show the other side to them as long as they are with their friends that are supposed to be "bad boys" too, so therefore they have to act baddish and thuggish. So you would see that a lot of them would come and dance with you at a gay club, want to kiss you, or want to actually fuck you, but when you pass them on the street, you cannot approach them.' Omar did not have a problem with this last component of public behaviour. Throughout our conversations he stressed the importance of being discreet in public. 'If you know who you are, you don't have to publicize it for the whole world to know, understand me? You could be gay, and I could be gay, and I could greet you on the street, and no one has to know that I am all with this woman and you are all with that woman, right?' Omar reminded me at this point of my embarrassing failure to pass with that 'broke wrist' (floppy wrist) action, the overly tight shirt, and short shorts that 'screamed buller,' when we had visited his sister in the country a few weeks before.

In these discussions with Omar about public conduct, respect repeatedly arose as an important factor in social exchanges, echoing the narratives of and about queens in chapter 5, although the assessment of and criteria for displaying and earning respect were not identical. For example, according to Omar, discretion was a way of respecting the other person and of not embarrassing them or oneself in a public setting. If two men shared the knowledge that they were gay, then if they respected each other, they would be very discreet about this knowledge and certainly not draw any untoward attention to themselves if they met in public. For Omar, respect was a fundamental principle of social relations in Barbadian society: 'All in all, all of us have our respect – the church has its own respect, the gay community has its respect, the average person has their own respect … so therefore at the end of the day it's all about giving respect where respect is due.' Omar felt that because of the societal emphasis on respect, Barbados was more tolerant towards gays than was Jamaica. He felt that Barbadian society was becoming more tolerant of homosexuality and that there were more men now who were like him (that is, who did not pretend by having wives and girlfriends). In fact, Omar believed that in twenty years 'there will be people actually being able to come and tell their dad and their mum, "I am gay, and this is my lover, and he is staying for the weekend."'

When I first met Omar, he was keen to accompany me to the various bars and clubs around the island where local men were known to meet. As noted in chapter 4, most of these bars were in tourist areas, and the majority of clientele were white tourists, but for at least one night each week local gay men and some women would show up in small groups and occupy a section of the club or bar. However, from 2004 onwards Omar was less interested in spending time in these spots; he told me that it was boring because he always saw the same old tired faces, and he also did not have the money to spend on drinks. But I do not think that Omar was telling me the whole story. As mentioned above, by 2004 Omar had begun to attend a Seventh-day Adventist church that appeared to be influential in changing his opinion on the acceptability of being gay or of the gay 'lifestyle,' as he now sometimes referred to it. More of his free time was dedicated to church-sponsored social events like reading groups, picnics, and informal gatherings at the homes of fellow church members. I asked him if there were other closeted queens at these informal gatherings, and he replied that he did not think so and that he was not interested if there were.

Nevertheless, during my visit with him in 2008, he enthusiastically accepted an invitation to a private gay and lesbian party being held at a rented hall near Bridgetown and, within forty minutes of arriving, had retreated into nearby bushes with a newfound male friend.

Michael

I also met Michael and Terry (Michael's partner) through Edward, who had worked with Terry in the hospitality industry on a couple of occasions. When I asked Michael about his upbringing, he told me that he was born in 1974 in a rural area located in the north end of the island, but he grew up in St James (the parish immediately northwest of Bridgetown), which is known as 'the gay capital of Barbados ... You drop a twenty-five-cent piece in St James, you got to kick it all the way to Bridgetown, because every man in St James is gay and there's no exception to the rule!' Michael told me that he was the youngest in his family and 'from a poor background'; both of his parents had working-class jobs. His grandparents, an uncle and aunt, and his cousins all lived on the same family plot, so it was like a big family with the kids all raised together, mainly by the grandmother. Michael clearly remembered hearing his mother talk disparagingly about buller men in his neighbourhood. From early on, he remembered neighbourhood children calling him a she-she because he was effeminate, quiet, and did not like playing sports.

Michael heard many more of these remarks when he began attending secondary school, where he said he felt further intense pressure to conform, to behave like a 'typical' boy, while at the same time recognizing that he was sexually attracted to boys. 'It was probably the time that I tried hardest to be straight ... but I was harassed right from the beginning because I didn't like sports, I wasn't rough, I didn't have a girlfriend or girlfriends like the others, so people were making nasty comments ... Others had it worse ... they were more effeminate. I learned to pass through school by taking authoritative positions like monitor, then prefect, then deputy head boy, so that helped keep people at bay when teachers weren't around.'

Michael said that the 'lowdown' thing was happening regularly at school, but he never got involved with anyone even though he had a reputation for being a buller. He remembered a particularly vicious young guy, 'the Jock,' from his school who picked on him regularly, but then one night at home, the phone rang, and it was the Jock. He said he understood that Michael was 'giving away all that,' and he wanted his share. 'I was shocked. One of the guys treating me the worst now telling me wants some!' Michael did not agree to the Jock's request.

Michael's first real experience with a young man was in his final year at his secondary school when he went on a school trip to another Caribbean island. He met a guy from there, and 'we fell for each other ... We kissed, and it felt really good, so from then I decided, "Hey, you know, here is what I am."' They stayed in touch for years, and even after his friend married, he continued to write and call Michael, reminding him that 'it's better over here!' After this affair Michael became more interested in getting a boyfriend and found him one day when he was passing through the biggest department store in downtown Bridgetown, Cave Shepherd. 'Robert' saw Michael in the men's section, got his number from a mutual friend, and it went from there for two years. It was over these years (from the ages of sixteen to eighteen) that Michael started to socialize with other gay men: 'Even at school there were people who figured each other out, and we started to lime together.'

After Michael graduated from secondary school and attended community college to study science in the 1990s, he was surprised to find that life on the campus was just as rough for him as it had been in secondary school. 'You would have thought it would be better, [but] the pressure and harassment continued.' One of the worst incidents of his life occurred at college when he was sitting on the library steps and 'a group of men from the technology division came out of their building and started to call us names and threw cups of ice and things ... We were scared, so we got up and ran, and fortunately they didn't follow us to beat us up.' It was during his years at college that he met an older student in an English literature class who was divorced and had a daughter; the student thought 'he had me figured out ... and would always tell me that my lifestyle was unhealthy and no good.' One day their teacher took them to see the play *Equus*, which, as Michael said, was a very erotically charged production. Afterwards, the older student offered to drive Michael home but first invited him into his apartment for a drink. When they arrived at his place, the man went into his bedroom and told Michael to come in to see something. When he walked in, there was the man standing buck naked except for a red thong. Michael fooled around a bit with him, but he was not interested in someone 'who said one thing and then wanted another.'

Another place in which Michael felt he received mixed messages about homosexuality during his youth was the church. His family attended a Pentecostal church, and Michael was very active in the church throughout his youth as a choirboy, a Youth Fellowship member, and later a song director ('I was a fabulous song leader. I loved to bang that cymbal!'). He remembered many lectures from the pulpit about Sodom and Gomorrah and that 'if a man lies with a man, it is a sin that shall not be forgiven,' which made him very afraid. However, he found that by getting more involved in church activities, he was less harassed by family and friends because they thought he was 'involved in higher things ... So it was easier for me to be around men because they were all men of the church.' Michael explained that because religion was so powerful and popular in Barbados ('That's because God is a Bajan,' he joked), many gay men could participate in the church and use it to explain why they did not have a girlfriend and did not perform a 'normative' heterosexual masculinity that involved aggressive expressions of desire for and to women. 'I was surrounded by gay people in the church ... At one point I felt that being in the church was equated to being gay ... at least 50 per cent of the men in the chorale were gay ... You don't know it now, but there was something called the Nazarene Tabernacle, in Eagle Hall, where they used to have all the gospel concerts, and my mother allowed me to go because it was a gospel concert, not knowing that I was going there to meet up with my gay friends ...It was a melting pot of gay people back in the early nineties.'

By the time he was in his mid-twenties and had left home to live on his own, Michael was disillusioned with the church and its hypocrisy. 'How can they say God is love and you love me and at the same time there is so much hatred towards people who are gay?' He started to read more about the history of Christianity and discovered that 'they are responsible for some of the biggest atrocities ... and I was uncomfortable with a religion that says we are the ones – we are right and Muslims, Jews, and Buddhists are wrong.' Michael stopped going to church and then described himself as 'governed by a higher power that is social, not Christian, and definitely not institutional.'

Michael had been together and living with his current boyfriend for over ten years, making this the longest gay relationship that I knew of in Barbados. They met at a private party, and even though Michael had heard that Terry was a big flirt, he fell for him quickly. Terry also came from a poor background but now had his own business and was doing quite well financially. Michael felt that since meeting, he and Terry had both settled down; he now had a secure managerial job and was not 'out on the scene' as much as he used to be. However, a more domestic life with Terry did not necessarily translate to greater peace and quiet. They had been forced to leave their first domicile, a rented home in Bridgetown, because of constant harassment by local men: 'People were throwing coconut shells through our windows, yelling names; people next door were peeping out as we passed through ... Everyone in that neighbourhood was into our business ... and then the crime started, and that was the straw that broke the camel's back. I think we were targeted, because our house was robbed four or five times ... I think robbing us was a way to get us out.' They moved to another rented home, in a quiet block of houses located about a half-hour's drive from Bridgetown, and they had no problems at all with anyone, even after a couple of fairly big parties that got a bit loud (one neighbour called the police, but that had been the only incident in five years).

I asked Michael if he felt that life was more difficult for gay youth and men from poor or working-class backgrounds than for middle-class gays in Barbados, since he had some experience on both sides of the fence. Michael responded that there were a lot of self-esteem issues for those who came from poorer neighbourhoods, in part because they were frustrated that they did not have many choices. 'Some come out very crude, bombastic, or very flamboyant and like a girl … but you should not always think that because they're from a poor background, they are going to be loud, bombastic, and out there … You have to take in the parental upbringing.' However, Michael felt that among the younger set (men in their twenties) there was a new development of the 'thug' style: guys who act like they are on a rap video and say they do not want to have anything to do with 'fem' styles or effeminate men. Michael had no patience for all this 'pretending to be a real man' and saying they only want a 'real man': 'We are all gay. Face it.' He said this new style is very prevalent at all levels of society, and it is making gay men even more fearful about their sexuality because they worry that others will talk about how '"he went and did this and likes to do that, so he ain't a real man." … Things are not easy here in Barbados in the first place. It's a small space here, and you can feel claustrophobic … you worry about the gossip – who will it get to and what are people saying about you – and you don't want people to be nasty to your family.'

As Michael and Terry had travelled overseas a few times (to places like London, New York, and Toronto), I asked Michael if he had ever felt like moving to a place in which gays were more accepted, but his response was cautious:

> There's a degree of acceptance in those places, you feel less claustrophobic about who you are and what you are, and you don't have to worry about people getting in your business like here … There are certain streets there [where] you feel liberated, like on Church Street [in Toronto]; you feel like singing, 'This Land Is My Land' … but I also remember walking with some people from Toronto, and as soon as we left Church Street, they said, 'Let go he hand, let go he hand.'… People are just as prejudiced and can be just as cruel. I've been places in the [United] States where I was mighty scared and not sure if I should be in this neighbourhood, so we shouldn't go around fooling ourselves that homophobia only exists in small territories … It's out there and it's no different.

Tony

Tony was a long-time member of UGLAAB, and it was at one of their meetings in 2004 that we first met. Tony told me that he was forty-one years old, although I thought he looked much younger. He had grown up in a small town in the southern part of the island and still lived there with his mother. He had two younger brothers and 'some sisters from my father's side as far as I know,' owing to his father having left his mother at an early age and not maintaining contact. He had grown up 'without much of anything' because his mother did not earn much money at her various jobs (which included working at a res-taurant and as a maid at a hotel), and he did not like school much, so he had not done any post-secondary studies. Tony currently had two jobs, one as a security guard at a large house in a parish in the north, and the other at a store in Warrens, a suburb of Bridgetown, but he told me that his most interesting work experience occurred in rural Ontario, Canada, when he picked tobacco for a few seasons on the Labour Exchange Program[3] in 2000–1. When I asked Tony if he had come out to co-workers in any of his jobs, he replied, 'I don't talk about it, but I don't hide it.' He said he didn't hear any negative comments when he was working with other Bajan men on the farms in Ontario, but he had faced problems at the store in Warrens: 'As long as you're suspected as gay, you always have problems ... [but] as long as it's just talking, I have no problem with it.' He thought that most people had figured out he was gay, but they left him alone, except for one co-worker who came up to him one day and said, 'Man, what you watching me for?' to which Tony replied that this could only mean that the man was looking at him just as much, which shut him up.

Tony knew he was gay since he was nine years old, when he had an 'encoun-ter' with a friend of his younger brother, but he never had a conversation with another known gay man until he was twenty-five. His first 'real' sexual experi-ence took place at the age of eleven, with another boy who was a year younger than Tony; it continued on and off for about ten years until his 'friend' went to prison ('he was always a problem child'), and they had since lost touch. Tony did not remember anyone saying anything good about homosexuality when he was growing up: 'I don't remember hearing about it in the Anglican church, [but] I remember hearing about it on the streets ... Boys on the street would say, "Bulla man up on the road. Don't go by he, he gonna try hold on pon yuh" ... People believe that cuz you're homosexual you're gonna wanna bung up with them or do their children ... that's so sick!'

Tony said that he grew up being scared of people knowing he was gay, so he did not want to come out to anyone; however, when he was about thirty years old, he was 'pushed out' because he was caught in the middle of a 'session' by some local guys who came up the road and found them doing it in an aban-doned building not too far from his home. One of these guys went all over the area, telling everyone everything, 'so I was put upon ... and it was rough for my mother.' One night soon after this incident Tony was walking home from town, and some of these same fellas passed by him and started yelling, 'Stab him, she-she man.' He ignored them, but when he turned down the gap (road) to his house, 'all of a sudden I could hear rocks whistle past my head. I turn around and look, and there's five fellas coming at me with rocks ... I was in such a mess, I couldn't open my door ... but then I said to myself, "This is my house; ain't nobody running me from my house." There was a rock heap beside the house, so I started pelting rocks back at them, and they take off cuz they didn't expect me to do that, and after that I was left alone for awhile.'

Tony said that he then did not care who knew and who did not, and it was just following this incident that he started his most serious relationship with Marco, also known as Sheba, who was a drag queen. Tony said that he was as surprised as I was that he fell in love with a queen, because his other boyfriends had tended to be 'rough' (masculine), but he and Marco had been together for almost three years. He had met her 'on the street' (I had heard from others that Sheba was a sex worker, but Tony never mentioned this in our interviews), and things had gone well for two years, but they started to quarrel over the fact that Sheba liked to go out too much, and Tony felt that she 'was not focused on what she really wants ... To be honest with you, I'm still in love with her, but her behaviour ... I remember more than once I came home from work really, really tired, but she'd wanted to go and party ...' Tony enjoyed their time together and told me about some great parties that they went to; one of his favourites was the Ambassador Gala, a drag-queen beauty pageant. He enjoyed going out with Sheba because she loved getting attention, and much of it was not negative. Tony felt that Bajans were more accepting of queens than of gay men: 'There's a different attitude towards him [Sheba] ... People are more in shock than hostile; they don't know what to do ... One time we were walking through a crowd at a street party in Speightstown, and one of the guys, he said, "You, you ain' no woman," and Sheba turn, right in the middle of the crowd, an' kiss me and said, "I'm more woman than you'll ever get," and the crowd went wild. And the thing about it is, I can't remember hearing negative comments. Everybody knew Sheba was a queen, so it just goes to show, you never know what to expect.'

Tony felt that while queens were more accepted in public, things were getting worse for gays in Barbados, because 'we have more gay people coming out and saying, "This is who I am," and they are coming out just as men – they are not so queenish like back in the day – and because of this, a lot of men are questioning their own identity. So they have a problem with this ... it makes them nervous and lash out.' I told Tony that I had not seen any examples of men 'coming out' in Barbados; at least, I had not come across any man who was fully out to all friends, family members, and workers, but Tony responded that it was true: 'These days you will see regular guys (and not just the flamboyant ones) being more open. They will come up to each other and talk on the street, which they had not done twenty years ago.' When I asked Tony to explain why more gay men were coming out if he felt that there was more homophobia in Barbados today, he repeated his argument that more out gay men were contributing to the homophobic reactions by other men.[4] In addition to there being more out, regular gay men, Tony thought that another factor contributing to the worsening situation was the increased popularity of Jamaican dance-hall and dub music styles, with their homophobic lyrics. In addition, he said, 'Bajans talk too much ... People start spreading rumours out of jealousy or to take the heat off themselves.'

When I returned to Barbados in 2008, I visited the UGLAAB office and spoke with a few of the members whom I had met in 2004. Tony was not among them, and when I asked where he was, I was told that he had not been coming to meetings in a while. I asked one of the members who knew Tony if he knew where I might find him, but he told me that Tony probably would not want to talk to me because he was not talking to anyone much 'since Sheba was killed last year.' He then pulled out a folder with some newspaper articles and a memorial-service program. According to the newspaper, Sheba had been killed by her boyfriend (not Tony) during a domestic dispute. The boyfriend was now in jail, facing charges of homicide. In the program Sheba was identified by both his birth and drag names, and Tony was listed as one of the speakers reciting a passage from the Bible.

Conclusion: Flaming Souls and Imperial Debris

On 25 July 2009, the *Nation* newspaper published an article titled 'Drag Queens on Show,' which announced that eight queens from Barbados and Trinidad would be vying for the title of Miss Galaxy World in an upcoming beauty pageant to be organized by Darcy Dear, founder of UGLAAB, to raise funds for people living with HIV/AIDS. On the *Nation*'s website, readers could post responses to the article, and, perhaps not too surprisingly, within a week of the article's publication there were over sixty postings, of which approximately 75 per cent were negative or critical and 25 per cent were neutral or supportive.[1] The critical comments echoed sentiments that were similar to those discussed in chapter 1, with an emphasis on the dangers to Barbados of supporting this kind of un-Christian, decadent lifestyle, that a drag-queen show was a sure sign of an increase in general social depravity and sin, and that this was further evidence of gays pushing their agenda down people's throats. What seemed particularly offensive to the naysayers was the public visibility of the event because it was being announced in the national newspaper with a date, location, brief description of events, and no proscriptive comments. As one commentator put it, 'Keep your homosexuality to yourself ... When you put it on public display, you have crossed the line.'

Although we are not told exactly what line is being crossed, I think it might well have something to do with respectability, a theme that has emerged repeatedly throughout this book. As we have seen, respectability is an important and complex value in Barbados, operating across multiple spaces and registers and thus freighted with potentially diverse meanings for the same individual in different contexts. As I have documented throughout these chapters, in the public spaces, airwaves, and pages of Barbados respectability is often linked to discourses of good citizenship, national identity, and character. Homosexuality is generally not a category associated with respectability in these contexts; if anything, it would appear that the homosexual represents the exact opposite. He (as we have seen, the male homosexual is the focus of most public talk) is a threat to the norm of respectable citizenship; his perceived effeminate presence is an improper assemblage of sexual and gendered desires, kinaesthetics, and demands, which, to some, threatens the order and organization of the post-colonial heteropatriarchal nation state that is fighting an uphill battle on the masculinist stage of neoliberal global capitalism.

However, we have also seen that in Barbados there is awareness that this particular version of respectable citizenship is nothing more than a garment in the emperor's wardrobe of new clothes; like the vain king of Hans Christian Andersen's tale who believes that his new clothes are made from a fabric that is too fine and elegant for the masses to perceive until a child cries out that he is naked, in numerous sectors of Bajan public and private life a long-standing critique of the rules of this version of respectable citizenship render its power ambivalent, if not naked at certain moments. Returning to the news item above, among those who wrote in support of the Miss Galaxy World event, many noted the hypocrisy of the commentators who presented Christian moral values as the foundation of their critique. Some asked why only homosexuals were being condemned, when Barbados was full of adulterers, thieves, liars, and other sinners according to Christian moral codes. Another letter writer asked how these upright Christians could condemn homosexuals when their churches were known to be full of them. Others utilized excerpts from the Bible to counterbalance those who claimed that homosexuality was a sin (for example, 'Let he who has not sinned cast the first stone'), and a few supporters argued that drag queens had 'the right' to organize a pageant because Barbados was a free country where citizens could exercise freedom of speech and expression. In these comments we see similar themes to those of the narratives of Bajan queens and gay men presented in chapters 5 and 7, in which accusations of hypocrisy, deception, and contradictory behaviour were aimed at any Bajan (of any socio-economic standing or sexual persuasion) who declared herself or himself to have the moral authority to proclaim what was right and wrong. We also see the discourse of rights (albeit in the framework of liberal individualism) emerging once again as a strategy of contestation.

The critique of this version of respectability, alongside the ongoing centrality of its value as an important component of social acceptability and individual worth, is often located in one and the same person. In other words, it is not simply the case that we can group supporters and detractors of respectability by socio-economic, political, age-based, gendered, or sexual status. Earning, keeping, and showing respect is valued by Bajans across the socio-economic spectrum, but equally valued is the ability to recognize, and in certain contexts embrace, the tensions, discrepancies, gaps, and contradictions of trying to maintain and perform a particular version of respectable life.

For many Bajans, especially those who are rendered marginal by the powerful heteropatriarchal norms and regulations of the nation state, there is thus what we might call a strategic engagement with hegemonic forms of respectability, a carefully and complexly formed relationship to the version of respectable values that is articulated in domains of public authority like the newspaper, the government-sponsored public forum, and the religious pulpit. This strategic engagement is produced through the historical experiences of the racialized colonial subject who is located in a society where, in the past, colonial administrators worked very hard to establish and maintain a rigorous hierarchy of social inequality, in part through an ontology premised on the impossibility of the colonized subject to attain moral worth equivalent to that of the colonizer. Thus, in colonial societies like Barbados the racialized subject could never be as educated, civilized, and morally upstanding – in other words, *respectable* – as the white European who ruled him or her. One strategy employed to challenge this exclusionary matrix of power was to outdo the master at his own game, that is, to be more pious, civilized, educated, and socio-politically organized, using the civic, legal, and moral codes of the colonizer's institutions. Another strategy was to develop and adhere to beliefs and credos that differed in form, relation, and practice from the Euro-American moral frameworks of the colonizers because they drew on memories, words, practices, and rituals of different times and places and stood in opposition to the discriminatory structures that oppressed and excluded. Respectability was an important component of these divergent beliefs and practices as well, but it was established through different calculations and standards.

Gender and sexuality were, and continue to be, central components of colonial and post-colonial nationalisms, which, as George Mosse and many others have pointed out, are very much invested in respectability (Mosse 1985; Alexander 2005). Since the nineteenth century (and until very recently in a few nations) the homosexual has been a symbol of danger, degeneration, or death in the heteropatriarchal respectable nationalisms of most nation states. In post-colonial societies, where the racialized male citizen has been historically rendered as sexually dangerous, promiscuous, or impotent, and excluded from any significant institution of political or economic power, a countering discourse of respectable Afro-Bajan masculinity, emphasizing education, heterosexual marriage, a nuclear family, community leadership, economic independence, and adherence to Christianity was developed prior to and following independence from Britain, but this formation of masculinity emulated many of the dominant features of the normative white middle-class masculinity in the colonizing nation. The tensions inherent in potentially reproducing oppressive and exploitative structures of power have been experienced by many (albeit to different degrees depending on the distance from that norm, calculated through the intersection of racial, gendered, sexual, and classed subjectivities), hence the persistent claims of hypocrisy, deceit, and deception that coexist with the development of other modes of defining, acting, and being respectable.

The homosexual, long vilified in the hetero-nationalisms of colonizing nation states, was unlikely to be included in post-independence Bajan discourses of respectable national citizenship. However, as we have seen in the latter half of this book, queens and bullers have been visible and present in Bajan neighbourhoods for a very long time; they have been part of everyday life in homes, streets, shops, and bars throughout Barbados. The queens, with their blatant non-conformity and disregard for the rules of middle-class heteropatriarchal respectable citizenship, appear to have been respected in certain contexts by many of their fellow community members, just as non-marital sexual relations, serial monogamy or polyamory, non-nuclear families, women as breadwinners, alternative economic arrangements and formations, and different relationships to spiritual worlds have also been accepted as viable, sensible, or necessary components of social life. In these beliefs and relations lay another matrix or calculus through which respectability was earned and kept, and some of the queens were able to earn and keep a respectable status, albeit alongside a reputation for being fierce and able to verbally and physically defend themselves when necessary.

However, since the 1980s – when the scourge of HIV/AIDS was mistakenly attributed solely to homosexual sex, activism for lesbian and gay (and now queer) rights gradually shifted from local to global levels (such that some nations eventually supported a middle-class white version of gay citizenship) (Puar 2007; Valentine 2007), and evangelical Christian religious organizations (many of which are based in the United States and/or have strong affiliations with American counterparts) increased their presence in the Caribbean – the symbolic capital of the homosexual in Barbados (as well as many other nation states around the world) has shifted from ambivalent street-level respectability to the halls, corridors, and pages that produce and regulate the discourses of respectable citizenship of the nation state; these locations were predicated upon the colonial order of things, an order that was and still is deeply racialized, classed, and heteropatriarchal. Furthermore, we now live in an era of blinding mobility of capital, in which the effects of new formations and movements of global capitalism are producing a new global ecumene with fewer, wealthier owners and many more underpaid or unemployed workers. As I argued in chapter 1, the language, actions, and effects of global capitalism are deeply heteropatriarchal, and the labour of workers in service economies has become materially and metaphorically feminized.[2] As we have seen, for some Bajans, the homosexual's attempt to move from the realm of the illicit (where, Bajans will often admit, he can be amusing as long as he knows his place) into the space of national respectability as a citizen with rights is an attempt to legitimize effeminate masculinity and thus threatens the 'natural' (that is, heteropatriarchal) order of society.

The effects of this symbolic shift of the homosexual from street to state respectability are being negotiated in media, pulpits, courts, and parliamentary halls of nation states around the world. However, in societies formed through the crucible of colonization (whether they be colonizing or colonized), the production and regulation of respectable citizenship (which always includes racialized, classed, gendered, and sexual components) by the nation state continues to be affected by what Anne Stoler identifies as 'imperial debris.' Stoler notes that imperial formations are unlike empires in that they are processes of becoming; they are not fixed things. They are defined by racialized allocations, appropriations, and relations of force harbouring political forms that endure beyond the formal exclusions that legislate against equal opportunity, commensurate dignities, and equal rights. Quoting Martinican writer Edouard Glissant, she observes that 'in these imperial formations the dominated must search elsewhere for the principle of domination because the system of domination is not directly tangible' (2008, 193–4). In other words, the struggle to emerge from under the shackles of colonial rule does not easily or immediately result in the dismantling of multiple and intersecting social, economic, and political hierarchies, which are always in flux owing to economic, political, and technological transformations on local and global scales. While relatively new independent nation states like Barbados may now articulate a liberal discourse of equality for all citizens, this does not necessarily mean that the effects of racialized heteropatriarchy, formed through the historical dialectic of empire and colony, will be fundamentally challenged or altered. While the racialized component of respectable citizenship in the nationalist discourses of Barbados may have significantly transformed since independence from Britain in 1966[3] (in which respectability is precisely *not* about becoming white even while it is premised on appropriating the qualities of former imperial rulers into a postcolonial black diasporic form), the gendered and sexual component has not transformed; this is evidence of the imperial debris of nineteenth- and early-to-mid-twentieth-century Euro-American nationalist formations. Homosexuality was profoundly antithetical to these nationalisms, and the homophobia found in numerous contemporary nationalisms around the globe can be viewed as one piece of debris of these imperial formations. However, homosexuality and homophobia operate in different registers in the post-colonial nationalisms of the African diaspora. The arguments against the rights of homosexuals in some twenty-first-century nation states like Barbados are responses to new forms of economic and political imperialism that, despite their rhetoric of economic freedom and individual liberty, perpetuate the structural economic and political inequalities that were created in the colonial era, carrying forward powerful and deeply problematic binary metaphors of civilized-uncivilized, developed-developing, and first-third nationalisms, which are manifested through gendered, classed, sexual, and racial hierarchies.

In other words, the system of domination has simultaneously shifted yet remained the same; the direct, tangible structure of colonial power has been replaced by the no less powerful but more diffuse and complex effects of global capital restructuring and new transnational political-economic alliances that simultaneously build on and transform older imperial orders and their attendant organization of gendered, sexualized, classed, and raced hierarchies. In these newer imperial formations, the homosexual is no longer universally vilified; in some nation-state discourses a particular racialized and classed version of the homosexual (white, middle-class, and married) is now held aloft as a model citizen, often in comparison to the less 'civilized' (that is, homophobic) nationalisms of the global South, in order to justify heightened national security and militarism (see Puar 2007 for a trenchant critique of this form of homo-nationalism). However, in other hegemonic nationalist discourses, often but not always found in former colonies whose economies are increasingly service oriented and locked into the interests of the neoliberal policies of global capitalism, and where there are large segments of the population who are increasingly struggling to make ends meet, there are some who cannot envision any version of the homosexual as a figure of national respectability, particularly when he is identified with a form of progressive modernity that is located in and associated with imperial formations of citizenship that are also identified as hegemonically white, and thus they have come to identify him as the bogeyman of the new global order.

Yet, as I have argued above, respectability's power has never been stable in Barbados; there has always been more than one way to be respectable, and certainly more than one way to critique it. The normative order of middle-class heterosexuality, patriarchy, and Christian religious orthodoxy has never been fully secure because many women, some men, and the more visible queens have consistently ignored or contested aspects of its regulative intent. From the days of the plantation to the present there have been multiple, fluid, and shifting social, economic, and moral practices operating in Barbados, affecting hegemonic discourses of respectable citizenship, so that these discourses do not sit in as stable a position as they do in settler states like the United States, where the moral codification of white heteropatriarchy has established a stranglehold on sociopolitical and economic order. In a society where the majority of citizens are racialized, connected to a history of enslavement and colonization, and/or economically marginalized, official norms and orders of the nation state are simultaneously more stringent and more unstable, rendering the operations of these orders and their effects opaque, unstable, and nebulous. Furthermore, technology, new movements of global capital, and transnational political-economic alliances may simultaneously intensify and destabilize normative racialized heteropatriarchal orders. While for some citizens the effects of these mobilizations may be rendering their nation state increasingly weak and vulnerable (that is, feminized) on the global stage, for others these same forces may be producing new desires, relationships, and identities, as illustrated in chapter 6 where we saw that the increased presence and use of cellphones, texting, and cheap regional Caribbean calling plans facilitated new romantic relationships between some Bajan queens and Jamaican men. Another illustration of the unpredictable convergences of desire, capital, and politics can be seen in the rise of gay tourism (discussed in chapter 4), which simultaneously destabilizes older tropes of heteronormative modernity while re-inscribing racialized hierarchies through comparative talk of 'civilized' versus 'uncivilized' societies, evaluated in terms of an ethnocentric definition of homosexual liberation.

Darcy Dear told me that the 2009 Miss Galaxy World beauty pageant was a success and went off without a hitch; the audience was large and supportive, and so more pageants were being planned. A few weeks after the pageant, I received a call from Omar, inviting me to his wedding. When I asked who was the groom, he replied that her name was Sandra and that she was a woman whom he had met at his new church (see chapter 7). In response to my surprised reaction (in which I think I sputtered out something like 'Why?'), Omar said that this was right for him and that 'she's the one.' They were going to live in his father's house after taking a honeymoon to Grenada. He was then going to look for a new job because he was tired of stacking and counting merchandise.

I end with Omar's wedding and the success of the Miss Galaxy World pageant because they are events that encapsulate, for me, the uneven, opaque, multiple, and nebulous effects of the debris of imperial formations in an age of globalization and the concomitant impossibility of complete new world orders. While some Bajan subjects adjust their gendered and sexual appearances, performances, and even preferences to conform to powerful nationalist discourses of heteropatriarchal respectability, others do not, or at least they make contextual adjustments. These are strategic engagements produced in and through a society in which the effects of colonialism, slavery, racism, patriarchy, material exploitation, forced migration, and diverse moral codes have generated multiple arrangements of sociality and individual worth, and individuals make different choices from among these arrangements depending on the moment, location, and relationship to people occupying a particular space at a particular time.

While queer activists in Europe and North America are increasingly focusing on the rights of sexual minorities around the globe and in many cases are advocating for change through similar pathways to those that were successful at home (that is, legal and constitutional challenges, international rights legislation, and local support or advocacy groups), there must be sensitivity and adjustment to the complex and divergent local contemporary contexts in which gendered and sexual desires are organized and regulated. In places like Barbados, the external support and pressure of queer activists located in the metropolitan centres of the North may create as many complications as they do solutions because their efforts are always entangled in the ruinous debris of imperial formations.

Notes

Introduction

1 *LGBTTIQQ2S* stands for 'lesbian, gay, bisexual, transgender, transsexual, intersex, queer, questioning, 2 spirited.'
2 Pride Toronto, accessed 13 August 2009, www.pridetoronto.com/festival/human-rights/.
3 Copenhagen 2009 World Outgames, 'Conference on Human Rights,' accessed 13 August 2009, www.copenhagen2009.org/home/conference/.
4 Human Rights Watch, 'Together. Apart,' accessed 17 August 2009, www.hrw.org/en/node/83161/section/2.
5 Barbados Statistical Service, www.barstats.gov.bb/census, accessed 7 September 2011.
6 I am using this term, *imagined*, with Benedict Anderson's (2006) arguments about imagined communities in mind.
7 Most references are to male homosexuality in public contexts (see below and chapter 2 for more on the reason for this).
8 See Alexander 2005, Padilla 2007, and Puar 2001 and 2002 for important exceptions to this argument.
9 Dennis Altman's writings (2001) on the spread of a global gay identity are, perhaps unfairly, presented by many as a primary illustration of this tendency (see for example Binnie 2004 and Cruz-Malave and Manalansan 2002).

1. The Spectral Homosexual in Barbadian Feedback Media

1 The report noted that there are laws in the Criminal Code of Barbados that are interpreted as anti-homosexual. However, as some legal analysts have pointed out, it could be argued that homosexuality is not illegal in Barbados; only certain

sexual actions or positions are (see chapter 2 for a more extensive discussion of the ambiguities of these sections of the Criminal Code). Nevertheless, the report advocated for the removal of these laws.

2 There was one feature article in the *Nation* consisting of an interview with the president of the group United Gays and Lesbians Against Aids in Barbados (UGLAAB) in which the president acknowledged that he was gay, but I do not include this because I am focusing on opinion or feedback media. See chapter 5 for more discussion on UGLAAB's president.

3 In December 2001, UGLAAB was formed to promote HIV/AIDS education, to eliminate discrimination against lesbians and gays with HIV/AIDS, and to defend the rights of persons living with HIV/AIDS. UGLAAB has organized informal discussion groups in Bridgetown, HIV/AIDS prevention workshops, and other outreach programs throughout the island. Their president at that time (2003) told me that while the group was dedicated to fighting for lesbian and gay rights, it was primarily focused on the impact of HIV/AIDS on the gay and lesbian community in Barbados.

4 I have given this letter writer a pseudonym.

5 See note 1 above.

6 While some callers and writers stated explicitly that Barbados is a Christian nation, others spoke of the lack of morality (or of moral decay) occurring throughout the nation and would then refer to the Bible as the source of proper morality, thus implicating national identity with Christian values.

7 As can be seen from the above examples, most discussions of homosexuality focus on sex between men. Lesbians are notably absent from the majority of this media talk. I address this absence below.

8 http://www.state.gov/r/pa/ei/bgn/26507.htm (accessed 21 November 2005).

9 See, for example, Prime Minister (and Finance Minister) Owen Arthur's 'The Economic and Financial Policies of the Government of Barbados,' presented on 14 March 2007, http://www.nationnews.com/www/budget/budget07.pdf (accessed on 5 October 2007).

10 These are tentative observations building on Freeman's analysis (2000) of changes to the Barbadian economy in the 1980s and 1990s. More research on the organization of and relations between male and female labour in the service industries is necessary in order to validate these observations.

11 This is not to suggest that female homosexuality is absent from the public imagination. Indeed, I heard a number of jokes and comments about prominent female politicians and other public figures in informal conversations with residents of Joyce's neighbourhood and members of UGLAAB, but these comments and jokes did not appear in the feedback-media discussions, possibly owing to the fact that these are considered 'respectable' public spaces. More theoretical work is neces-

sary in order to understand better the conditions that enable the appearance of such an absence in some sectors of Barbadian public culture and not in others.

12 Barbados is by no means entirely Christian. The 2000 census recorded 1,657 Muslims, 2,859 Rastafarians, 1,293 belonging to other 'Non-Christian' denominations, and 43,245 people who listed themselves as having no religious affiliation (or at least none listed on the census) (Barbados Statistical Service 2000, 34).

13 According to another source, many poorer Barbadians go to the Methodist and Moravian churches as well as to older Pentecostal churches (Nazarene, Pilgrim Holiness) in addition to those of Seventh-day Adventists, Jehovah Witnesses, and the Salvation Army. The claim that the Anglican Church is the dominant church in Barbados may thus reflect a hegemonic respectable middle-class discourse (www. trivester.com/churchers/barbados/all/, accessed 7 September 2011)

14 Further research is necessary on the organization of these media corporations. Owners, managers, and editors of Barbadian media make decisions about who and what goes into print and onto airwaves and computer and television screens. They may make their choices based on their own political and ideological agendas or on what they perceive to be their readership's position. The negative positioning of the homosexual in Barbadian media does not reflect a consistent, uniform trait of a culturally homogenous nation, so we must continue to examine the reason that this appears to be so, and we must challenge such claims to veracity.

2. Gender, Sexuality, and HIV/AIDS Discourses in Barbados

1 www.hivaidsbarbados.com (accessed on 14 July 2007).

2 www.census.gov (accessed on 20 May 2007).

3 www.unaids.org/en/Regions_Countries (accessed on 21 May 2007).

4 http://data.unaids.org/pub/EpiReport/2006/2006_epiupdate_en.pdf?preview=true (accessed on 24 May 2007).

5 www.carec.org/documents/Caribbean_HIV/AIDS_Epidemic.pdf (accessed on 24 May 2007).

6 One such law states, 'Any person who commits buggery is guilty of an offence and is liable on conviction on indictment to imprisonment for life' (Barbados Sexual Offences Act, chapter 154).

7 Based on this comment, it was not clear whether gay and bisexual men were viewed by the Committee as vectors of disease or as having a right to health.

8 www.HIV/AIDSbarbados.com (accessed August 2007).

3. Whose Right? Human and Sexual Rights Discourses in Barbados

1 The fourth way of reading rights according to Chambers is 'ressentiment,' where

the claim for rights can be understood not as a specifically political demand but as a moralizing claim, based on a history of prior injury. This claim instantiates in the law the very minority status of the group (2003, 149).

2 Accessed on 6 September 2011.

3 Accessed on 30 August 2005.

4 As Cowan and others have pointed out, while the idea of choosing (or not choosing) one's culture is appealing, it is also not reflective of many people's realities, in which the choice to belong or not belong is severely curtailed owing to one's location within and/or surveillance by powerful political, economic, and/or religious institutions (Cowan 2006, 15).

5 This is not to say that homosexual practices do not exist in Zimbabwe; as Engelke points out, they do, but they are not organized or labelled in the same way (1999, 302).

6 Chambers notes that the Bush II administration in the United States was actively trying to change the laws pertaining to reproductive choice and that, in many states, women were losing their rights to reproductive choice, rights that were instantiated in law over twenty years ago.

7 In Barbados these ranged from black self-help organizations that existed well before the twentieth century (such as the landship and burial societies) to the nationwide labour movement that arose in the 1930s and 1940s, which were dedicated to redressing the colonial legacy of social, economic, and political inequality faced by the majority of Barbadians (Beckles 1990, 151–85).

4. Gay Tourism and the 'Civilized' Homosexual

1 www.wikipedia.org (accessed on 3 March 2005).

2 I spoke with approximately thirty gay-identified Barbadian men on the topics of the social networks of local gay men and the relations between local and foreign gay men. Nine of these men participated in formal interviews (taped, in-depth conversations utilizing a set questionnaire). Some of these men I had met through Edward, others had been introduced to me by Joyce, my friend in Bridgetown, and still others had been met in Internet chat rooms or through mutual friends living in Toronto. These men ranged in age from twenty-three to forty-three years. Their occupations ranged from stock boy to government bureaucrat to waiter to computer engineer; all interviewees except for one had travelled overseas to North America, England, or other Caribbean islands at least once in their lives. Chapter 7 focuses in greater detail on some of these men's lives.

3 As Georgi observes, the use of the homosexual as a marker of civilized society is a relatively recent and somewhat contested development in nationalist and international development discourses.

5. Bajan Queens, Nebulous Scenes

1 Throughout this chapter I will use alternating gendered pronouns and adjectives (he, she; his, her) when discussing the queens as a means to more accurately represent their own shifting gendered and sexual self-descriptions between *gay* and *queen*. As I elaborate below, terms like *gay* and *transgendered* are problematic as sexual descriptors owing to their hegemonic Euro-American origins, which, when applied to the queens' narratives, do not comfortably embody these gendered or sexual subjectivities.

2 It should be noted that although women were present in many of the venues I visited such as UGLAAB or Darcy's bar, the majority of my interviewees were anatomically male, which means that this analysis of sexual diversity in Barbados reflects a gendered perspective, albeit one that is different from hegemonic heterosexual masculine discourses. Lesbian or female same-sex desires and relationships were clearly evident and should be further investigated because their subjectivities, relationships, and organization would contribute to more fully representing the complexity of Bajan sex-scapes.

3 Interestingly, one informant told me that the pageant was organized by a heterosexual married woman.

4 See Wilson (1973) for one of the first descriptions of this dynamic in the Caribbean. I will return to discuss respectability in more detail in the concluding chapter of this book.

5 This statement is based on my archival research of the *Nation*. I conducted a content analysis of the *Nation* for references to homosexuality since the daily newspaper's inception in 1973. I read every issue published from 1 September to 31 December in the years 1974, 1984, 1994, and 2004. While a couple of 1974 issues referred to homosexuals, the term *gay* first appeared in 1984 in reference to a gay man named as a judge in New York.

6 See Roderick Ferguson's description (2007) of 'black rural sissies' in rural Georgia in the 1970s for a similar description of gendered heterogeneity.

7 The perceptions, experiences, and opinions of gender-normative, gay-identified Bajan males are explored in greater detail in chapter 7, but it should be noted here that most of the gay-identified men whom I knew did not explicitly state that they feared being identified as queens. At the same time, certain characteristics of the effeminate queen were considered taboo behaviours from which these men tried to distance themselves as much as possible in public contexts. Robert, who identified as gay, told me to 'stop breaking' my wrists one day when we were having lunch at Chefette, a local fast-food chain restaurant. He felt that I was flopping my hands around too much as I talked, which was drawing suspicious looks from people at surrounding tables. For many self-identified gay Bajan males, the management

of gendered performativity, particularly in relation to clothing styles and physical movements, occupied a central role in the construction of their socio-sexual identity, and, while not stated explicitly, the effeminate queens such as Didi and Darcy likely operated as a sort of foil against which both gender-normative masculinity and homosexuality were evaluated.

6. Digisex: Cellphones, Barbadian Queens, and Circuits of Desire in the Caribbean

1 See Miller and Slater (2000) for a similar study of the use and significance of the Internet in Trinidad.
2 A chattel home was traditionally defined as a piece of movable property that could literally be picked up and put on a truck to be moved at a moment's notice, as these homes were built on land rented from someone else. Those who lived in chattel houses were considered to be poor because they could not afford to buy their own land. A chattel house was a small wood-framed structure, usually consisting of a living-dining room, a kitchen, and one or two bedrooms; however, many chattel homes may be smaller or larger, and there are now houses that are not considered to be chattel houses because they are made with high-quality, expensive greenheart wood.
3 I suspect Omar's sensitivity to my clothing choices was also heightened by the fact that he was being seen in public with a white male who looked like a tourist, a coupling that, I was told on other occasions, might signal to local Bajans a homosexual relationship because it was rare to see black males and white males socializing together in public venues like restaurants or shops.
4 Batson Savage provides an example of a partner who scrolls through recently made calls or address lists, looking for suspicious names and numbers.
5 Freeman's research goes on to interrogate the interesting question of why, among her middle-class informants, a much higher proportion (60 per cent) were married.
6 I neglected to ask the Jamaicans whether or not there existed a similar category of queens in Jamaica and, if so, whether their behaviours and relationships were organized in a similar way to those of the Bajans.

7. Life Stories

1 Informal discussions that focused on topics similar to those in the interviews took place with an additional twelve men.
2 Details about each interviewee's family, friends, lovers, work, and locations have been changed in order to ensure confidentiality.

3 Canada's Seasonal Agricultural Workers Program has been bringing workers in from the Caribbean to work on farms (mostly in Ontario) since the 1960s.

4 I think Tony and I were working with different definitions of *coming out*. Mine reflected a more mainstream gay North American semi-politicized interpretation, where coming out was an act of asserting a sexualized identity to society at large, that is, following a performative narrative in which this identity is claimed in any and all contexts. Tony's definition of *out gay men* referred to men who were now willing to claim their desire for men 'as men,' that is, as males following a normative performance of masculinity.

Conclusion: Flaming Souls and Imperial Debris

1 www.nationnews.com/print/drag-queen-show-copy-for-web (accessed on 5 August 2009.

2 Once again, it is important to reflect on the way in which feminization is being constructed in these global capital formations and in whose eyes feminization is a bad thing. In a heteropatriarchal political economy, feminization is problematic because it stands for disempowerment; however, from a feminist perspective, feminization of the economy could have very different meanings and outcomes based on principles of socio-economic equity, anti-discrimination, and gender parity.

3 See Thomas (2004) for a discussion of shifting definitions of race and nation in Jamaica.

References

Abdur-Rahman, Aliyyah. 2006. The Strangest Freaks of Despotism: Queer Sexuality in Antebellum African American Slave Narratives. *African American Review* 40 (2): 223–37.

Abrahams, Roger. 1983. *The Man of Words in the West Indies: Performance and the Emergence of Creole Culture*. Baltimore, MD: Johns Hopkins University Press.

Alexander, Jacqui M. 1994. Not Just (Any) Body Can Be a Citizen: The Politics of Law, Sexuality, and Postcoloniality in Trinidad and Tobago and the Bahamas. *Feminist Review* 48:5–23.

– 1997. Erotic Autonomy as a Politics of Decolonization: An Anatomy of Feminist and State Practice in the Bahamas Tourist Economy. In *Feminist Genealogies, Colonial Legacies, Democratic Futures*, 63–100, ed. M. Jacqui Alexander and Chandra Talpade Mohanty. New York: Routledge.

– 2005. *Pedagogies of Crossing: Meditations on Feminism, Sexual Politics, Memory, and the Sacred*. Durham, NC: Duke University Press.

Altman, Dennis. 2001. *Global Sex*. Chicago: University of Chicago Press.

Anderson, Benedict. 2006. *Imagined Communities: Reflections on the Origin and Spread of Nationalism*. London: Verso.

Appadurai, Arjun. 1996. Modernity at Large: Cultural Dimensions of Globalization. Minneapolis: University of Minnesota Press.

Asad, Talal. 2003. *Formations of the Secular: Christianity, Islam, Modernity*. Stanford, CA: Stanford University Press.

Babb, Florence. 2004. Sexual Cultures and Modernizing Projects. *American Ethnologist* 31 (2): 225–30.

Barbados Statistical Service. 2000. *Population and Housing Census*. Bridgetown, Barbados: Government Printing Department.

Barrow, Christine. 1988. Anthropology, the Family and Women in the Caribbean. In *Gender in Caribbean Development*, 156–9, ed. Patricia Mohammed and Catherine

Shepherd. Mona, Jamaica: University of West Indies Women and Development Studies Project.

– 1996. *Family in the Caribbean: Themes and Perspectives*. Kingston, Jamaica: Ian Randle Press. Barrow, Christine, and J.E. Greene. 1979. *Small Business in Barbados: A Case of Survival*. Cave Hill, Barbados: Institute of Social and Economic Research, University of West Indies.

Batson Savage, Tanya. 2007. 'Hol Awn Mek a Answer mi Cellular': Sex, Sexuality and the Cellular Phone in Urban Jamaica. *Continuum: Journal of Media and Cultural Studies* 21 (2): 239–51.

Beckles, Hilary. 1990. *A History of Barbados from Amerindian Settlement to Nation State*. Cambridge: Cambridge University Press.

Benyabib, Senya. 2002. *The Claims of Culture: Equality and Diversity in the Global Era*. Princeton: Princeton University Press.

Binnie, Jon. 2004. *The Globalization of Sexuality*. London: Sage Publications.

Boellstorff, Tom. 2003. Dubbing Culture: Indonesian Gay and Lesbi Subjectivities and Ethnography in an Already Globalized World. *American Ethnologist* 30 (2): 225–42.

– 2007. Queer Studies in the House of Anthropology. *Annual Review of Anthropology* 36: 17–35.

Butler, Judith. 1990. *Gender Trouble: Feminism and the Subversion of Identity*. New York: Routledge.

– 1993. *Bodies that Matter: On the Discursive Limits of Sex*. New York: Routledge.

Butler, Judith, Ernesto Laclau, and Slavoj Zizek. 2000. *Contingency, Hegemony, Universality: Contemporary Dialogues on the Left*. London: Verso.

Caribbean Community (CARICOM) Secretariat. n.d. *Charter of Civil Society for the Caribbean Community*. www.caricom.org. Accessed 29 October 2005.

Caribbean Telecommunications Union. 2007. http://www.ctu.int/ctu/AbouttheCTU/ MemberStates/Barbados/ tabid/93/Default.apx. Accessed 21 January 2008.

Chambers, Samuel. 2003. Ghostly Rights. *Cultural Critique* 54: 148–77.

Chevannes, Barry. 2001. *Learning to Be a Man: Culture, Socialization, and Gender Identity in Five Caribbean Communities*. Kingston, Jamaica: University of the West Indies Press.

– 2003. The Role of the Street in the Socialization of Caribbean Males. In *Gender and Sexuality in the Caribbean*, 215–33, ed. Linden Lewis. Gainesville: University Press of Florida.

Clift, Stephen, Michael Luongo, and Carrie Callister, eds. 2002. *Gay Tourism: Culture, Identity, and Sex*. New York: Continuum.

Collier, Jane, and Aihwa Ong. 2005. *Global Assemblages: Technology, Politics, and Ethics as Anthropological Problems*. Williston, ND: Blackwell Publishers.

Cowan, Jane. 2006. Culture and Rights after Culture and Rights. *American Anthropologist* 108 (1): 9–24.

Cowan, Jane, Marie Benedicte Dembour, and Richard A. Wilson, eds. 2001. *Culture and Rights: Anthropological Perspectives*. Cambridge: Cambridge University Press.

Crichlow, Wesley. 2004a. History, (Re)Memory, Testimony, and Biomythography: Charting a Buller Man's Trinidadian Past. In *Interrogating Caribbean Masculinities*, 185–224, ed. Rhoda Reddock. Kingston, Jamaica: University of West Indies Press.

– 2004b. *Buller Men and Batty Bwoys: Hidden Men in Toronto and Halifax Black Communities*. Toronto: University of Toronto Press.

Cruz-Malave, Arnoldo, and Martin Manalansan, eds. 2002. *Queer Globalizations: Citizenship and the Afterlife of Colonialism*. New York: New York University Press.

Dann, Graham. 1987. *The Barbadian Male: Sexual Attitudes and Practice*. London: Macmillan.

Eng, David. 2001. *Racial Castration: Managing Masculinity in Asian America*. Durham, NC: Duke University Press.

Engelke, Matthew. 1999. We Wondered What Human Rights He Was Talking About: Human Rights, Homosexuality, and the Zimbabwe Book Fair. *Critique of Anthropology* 19 (3): 289–314.

Ferguson, Roderick. 2004. *Aberration in Black: Toward a Queer of Color Critique*. Minnesota. University of Minnesota Press.

– 2007. Sissies at the Picnic: The Subjugated History of a Black Rural Queer. In *Feminist Waves, Feminist Generations: Life Stories of Three Generations in the Academy, 1968–1998*, ed. Hokulani Aikau, Karla Erickson, and Jennifer Pierce. Minneapolis: University of Minnesota Press.

Foucault, Michel. 1978. *The History of Sexuality*, Volume 1. New York: Pantheon Press.

Freeman, Carla. 2000. *High Tech and High Heels in the Global Economy*. Durham, NC: Duke University Press.

– 2001. Is Local: Global as Feminine: Masculine? Rethinking the Gender of Globalization. *Signs* 26 (4): 1007–37.

– 2007. Neoliberalism and the Marriage of Reputation and Respectability: Entrepreneurship and the Barbadian Middle Class. In *Love and Globalization: Transformations of Intimacy in the Contemporary World*, 3–37, ed. Mark Padilla, Jennifer Hirsch, Miguel Munoz-Laboy, Robert Sember, and Richard G. Parker. Nashville, TN: Vanderbilt University Press.

Freeman, Michael. 2004. The Problem of Secularism in Human Rights Theory. *Human Rights Quarterly* 26: 375–400.

Garber, Linda. 2003. One Step Global, Two Steps Back? Race, Gender, and Queer Studies. *GLQ* 10 (1): 125–8.

Giorgi, Gabriel. 2002. Madrid in Transito: Travelers, Visibility, and Gay Identity. *GLQ* 8 (1–2): 57–80

Glave, Thomas, ed. 2008. *Our Caribbean: A Gathering of Lesbian and Gay Writing from the Antilles*. Durham, NC: Duke University Press.

Gmelch, George, and Sharon Gmelch. 1997. *The Parish Behind God's Back: The Changing Culture of Rural Barbados*. Prospect Heights, IL: Waveland Press.

Goggin, Gerard. 2007. Introduction: Mobile Phone Cultures. *Continuum: Journal of Media and Cultural Studies* 21 (2): 133–5.

Goodale, Mark. 2006. Introduction to Anthropology and Human Rights in a New Key. *American Anthropologist* 108 (1): 1–8.

Gosine, Andil. 2004. Sex for Pleasure, Right to Participation, and Alternatives to AIDS: Placing Sexual Minorities and/or Dissidents in Development. IDRS Working Paper no. 228.

Gutzmore, Cecil. 2004. Casting the First Stone: Policy of Homo/Sexuality in Jamaican Popular Culture. *Interventions* 6 (1): 118–34.

Hage, Ghassan. 2000. *White Nation: Fantasies of White Supremacy in a Multicultural Society*. New York: Routledge.

Hall, Stuart. 1997. *Representation: Cultural Representations and Signifying Practices*. London: Sage Publications.

Henry, Anesta, and Sabrina Hall. 2004. Didi the Daring Diva. *The Nation*, 4 June, 18–19.

Henry, Frances, and Carol Tator. 2002. *Discourses of Domination: Racial Bias in the Canadian English Language Press*. Toronto: University of Toronto Press.

Hoad, Neville. 2007. *African Intimacies: Race, Homosexuality, and Globalization*. Minneapolis: University of Minnesota Press.

Horst, Heather. 2006. The Blessings and Burdens of Communication: Cell Phones in Jamaican Transnational Social Fields. *Global Networks: A Journal of Transnational Affairs* 6 (2): 142–60.

Horst, Heather, and Daniel Miller. 2006. *The Cell Phone: An Anthropology of Communication*. Oxford: Berg.

Howe, Alyssa Cymene. 2002. Undressing the Universal Queer Subject: Nicaraguan Activism and Transnational Identity. *City and Society* XIV (2): 237–79.

Hughes, Howard . 2002. Gay Men's Holiday Destination Choice: A Case of Risk and Avoidance. *International Journal of Tourism Research*, no. 4: 299–312.

Human Rights Watch. 2004. *Hated to Death: Homophobia, Violence, and Jamaica's HIV/AIDS Epidemic*. http://hrw.org/reports/2004/jamaica1104/ (accessed 14 June 2005).

Ivy, Marilyn. 1995. *Discourses of the Vanishing: Modernity, Phantasm, Japan*. Chicago: University of Chicago Press.

Jayawardena, Chandra. 1963. *Conflict and Solidarity in a Guianese Plantation*. London: Athlone Press.

Johnson, E. Patrick, and Mae Henderson, eds. 2005. *Black Queer Studies: A Critical Anthology*. Durham, NC: Duke University Press.

Jones, Vanessa Agard. 2009. Rights Revisited: Debating Sexual Politics in the French Caribbean. *Caribbean Review of Gender Studies*, no. 3. http://sta.uwi.edu/crgs/ (accessed 27 December 2009).

Justice, Daniel Heath. 2006. *Our Fire Survives the Storm: A Cherokee Literary History.* Minneapolis: University of Minnesota Press.

Kempadoo, Kamala. 2003. Sexuality in the Caribbean: Theory and Research (with an Emphasis on the Anglophone Caribbean). *Social and Economic Studies* 52 (3): 59–88.

– 2004. *Sexing the Caribbean: Gender, Race, and Sexual Labor*. New York: Routledge.

Kimmel, Michael. 2003. Globalization and Its Mal(e)contents. *International Sociology* 18 (3): 603–20.

Kulick, Don. 1998. *Travesti: Sex, Gender, and Culture among Brazilian Transgendered Prostitutes*. University of Chicago Press: Chicago.

Lafont, Suzanne. 2009. Not Quite Redemption Song: LGBT Hate in Jamaica. In *Homophobias: Lust and Loathing across Time and Space*, 105–22, ed. David A.B. Murray. Durham, NC: Duke University Press.

Lancaster, Roger. 1992. *Life Is Hard: Machismo, Danger, and the Intimacy of Power in Nicaragua*. Berkeley: University of California Press.

Lewis, Linden. 2003a. Caribbean Masculinity: Unpacking the Narrative. In *Gender and Sexuality in the Caribbean*, 94–128, ed. Lewis Linden. Gainesville: University Press of Florida.

– ed. 2003b. *The Culture of Gender and Sexuality in the Caribbean*. Gainesville: University Press of Florida.

Lovely, Bad. 2005. The Kings of Queens. *The Nation*, 4 February, 18.

Lyons, Andrew, and Harriet Lyons. 2004. *Irregular Connections: A History of Anthropology and Sexuality*. Lincoln: University of Nebraska Press.

Lyons, Harriet. 1999. The Representation of Trafficking in Persons in Asia: Orientalism and Other Perils. RE/Productions no. 2, http://www.hsph.harvard.edu/organizations/healthnet/SAsia/ejournals/ejournalsframe.html (accessed 4 March 2003).

MacCannell, Dean. 1976. *The Tourist: A New Theory of the Leisure Class*. New York: Schocken Books.

MacDonald, Myra. 2003. *Exploring Media Discourse*. Cornwall, UK: Arnold Publishers.

Mackey, Eva. 2002. *House of Difference: Cultural Politics and National Identity in Canada*. Toronto: University of Toronto Press.

Manalansan, Martin. 2003. *Global Divas: Filipino Gay Men in the Diaspora*. Durham, NC: Duke University Press.

Markowitz, Frances. 2004. Talking about Culture: Globalization Human Rights and Anthropology. *Anthropological Theory* 4 (3): 329–52.

Maxwell, James. 2004. A Culture of Bigotry. *Jamaica Observer*, 5 December. http://www.jamaicaobserver.com/ (accessed 12 June 2005).

Merry, Sally Engle. 2006a. *Human Rights and Gender Violence: Translating International Law into Local Justice*. Chicago: University of Chicago Press.

– 2006b. Transnational Human Rights and Local Activism: Mapping the Middle. *American Anthropologist* 108 (1): 38–51.

Miami Herald. 2007. Gay Travel Caribbean: Make Sure Islands Will Welcome You. 8 July, J4.

Miller, Daniel, and Don Slater. 2000. *The Internet: An Ethnographic Approach*. Oxford: Berg.

Mintz, Sidney. 1989. *Caribbean Transformations*. New York: Columbia University Press.

Mohammed, Patricia. 2003. A Blueprint for Gender in Creole Trinidad: Exploring Gender Mythology through Calypsos of the 1920s and 1930s. In *Gender and Sexuality in the Caribbean*, 129–68, ed. Linden Lewis. Gainesville: University Press of Florida.

Mosse, George. 1985. *Nationalism and Sexuality*. New York: H. Fertig.

Murray, David A.B. 2002. *Opacity: Gender, Sexuality, Race, and the 'Problem' of Identity in Martinique*. New York: Peter Lang Press.

National HIV/AIDS Commission of Barbados (NHAC). 2001. *The HIV/AIDS Epidemic: An Update*. Bridgetown, Barbados: National HIV/AIDS Commission.

Oswin, Neil. 2006. De-centring Queer Globalization: Diffusion and the Global Gay. *Environment and Planning D: Society and Space* 24: 777–90.

Padilla, Mark. 2007. *Caribbean Pleasure Industry: Tourism, Sexuality, and AIDS in the Dominican Republic*. Chicago: University of Chicago Press.

Padilla, Mark, Jennifer S. Hirsch, Miguel Munoz-Laboy, Robert Sember, and Richard G.Parker, eds. 2007. *Love and Globalization: Transformations of Intimacy in the Contemporary World*. Nashville, TN: Vanderbilt University Press.

Palmie, Stephan. 2006. Creolizaton and Its Discontents. *Annual Reviews in Anthropology* 35: 433–56.

Parker, Andrew, Mary Russo, Doris Sommer, and Patricia Yaeger, eds. 1992. *Nationalisms and Sexualities*. New York: Routledge.

Patton, Cindy. 1997. From Nation to Family: Containing African AIDS. In *The Gender/Sexuality Reader*, 279–90, ed. Roger Lancaster and Micaela DiLeonardo. New York: Routledge.

– 2002. *Globalizing AIDS*. Minneapolis: University of Minnesota Press.

Povinelli, Elizabeth A. 2002. *The Cunning of Recognition: Indigenous Alterities and the Making of Australian Multiculturalism*. Durham, NC: Duke University Press.

Prieur, Annick. 1998. *Mema's House, Mexico City: On Transvestites, Queens, and Machos*. Chicago: University of Chicago.

Puar, Jasbir Kaur. 2001. Global Circuits: Transnational Sexualities and Trinidad. *Signs* 26 (4): 1039–65.

– 2002. Introduction. *GLQ* 8 (1–2): 1–6.

– 2007. *Terrorist Assemblages: Homonationalism in Queer Times*. Durham, NC: Duke University Press.

Quiroga, Jose. 2000. *Tropics of Desire: Interventions from Queer Latino America*. New York: New York University Press.

Reddock, Rhoda. 1994. *Women, Labour, and Politics in Trinidad and Tobago: A History*. London: Zed Books.

– 2004. Interrogating Caribbean Masculinities: An Introduction. In *Interrogating Caribbean Masculinities: Theoretical and Empirical Analyses*, xiii–xxxiv, ed. Rhoda Reddock. Kingston, Jamaica: University of West Indies Press.

Robbins, Joel. 2004. The Globalization of Pentecostal and Charismatic Christianity. *Annual Review of Anthropology* 33: 117–43.

Rodriguez, Juana Maria. 2003. *Queer Latinadad: Identity Practices, Discursive Spaces*. New York: New York University Press.

Sen, Amartya. 2004. Elements of a Theory of Human Rights. *Philosophy and Public Affairs* 32 (4): 315–56.

Sharpe, Jenny, and Samantha Pinto. 2006. The Sweetest Taboo: Studies of Caribbean Sexualities; A Review Essay. *Signs* 32 (1): 247–74.

Slocum, Karla, and Deborah A. Thomas. 2003. Rethinking Global and Area Studies: Insights from Caribbeanist Anthropology. *American Anthropologist* 104 (3): 553–65.

Spitulnik, Debra. 1997. The Social Circulation of Media Discourse and the Mediation of Communities. *Journal of Linguistic Anthropology* 6 (2): 161–87.

Stoler, Anne Laura. 2008. Imperial Debris: Reflections on Ruins and Ruination. *Cultural Anthropology* 23 (2): 191–219.

Sullivan-Bloom, Constance. 2009. 'It's Adam and Eve, not Adam and Steve': What's at Stake in the Construction of Contemporary American Christian Homophobia. In *Homophobias: Lust and Loathing across Time and Space*, 48–63, ed. David A.B. Murray. Durham, NC: Duke University Press.

Thomas, Deborah A. 2004. *Modern Blackness: Nationalism, Globalization, and the Politics of Culture in Jamaica*. Durham, NC: Duke University Press.

Thomas, Deborah, and Kamari Clarke, eds. 2006. *Globalization and Race: Transformations in the Cultural Production of Blackness*. Durham, NC: Duke University Press.

Treichler, Paula. 1999. *How to Have Theory in an Epidemic: Cultural Chronicles of AIDS*. Durham, NC: Duke University Press.

United Nations General Assembly Special Session on HIV/AIDS. 2006. Country Report: Barbados. http://www.unaids.org/en/Regions_Countries (accessed 8 December 2007).

United Nations Office of the High Commissioner for Human Rights. n.d. *The Universal Declaration of Human Rights*. http://www.ohchr.org/EN/UDHR/Pages/Introduction.aspx (accessed 18 July 2005).

Valentine, David. 2007. *Imagining Transgender: An Ethnography of a Category*. Durham, NC: Duke University Press.

Van Dijk, Teuj A. 1988. *News as Discourse*. Hillsdale, NJ: Lawrence Erlbaum.

Walcott, Rinaldo. 2003. *Black Like Who? Writing Black Canada*. Toronto: Insomniac Press.

Walrond, E.R. (Mickey). 2004. Report on the Legal, Ethical, and Socio-economic Issues Relevant to HIV/AIDS in Barbados. Commissioned by the Attorney General's Office. Bridgetown, Barbados.

Wekker, Gloria. 1999. What's Identity Got to Do with it? Rethinking Identity in Light of the Mati Work in Suriname. In *Female Desires: Same Sex Relations and Transgender Practices across Cultures*, 119–38, ed. Evelyn Blackwood and Saskia Wieringa. New York: Columbia University Press.

– 2006. *The Politics of Passion: Women's Sexual Culture in the Afro-Surinamese Diaspora*. New York: Columbia University Press.

Whitehead, Tony. 1997. Urban Low Income African American Men, HIV/AIDS, and Gender Identity. *Medical Anthropology Quarterly* 11 (4): 411–47.

Williams, Petre. 2004. The Gay Debate. *Jamaica Observer*, 5 December.

Wilson, Peter. 1973. *Crab Antics: The Social Anthropology of English Speaking Negro Societies of the Caribbean*. New Haven, CT: Yale University.

Wright, Timothy. 2000. Gay Organizations, NGOs, and the Globalization of Sexual Identity: The Case of Bolivia. *Journal of Latin American Anthroplogy* 5 (2): 89–111.

Yingling, Thomas. 1997. *AIDS and the National Body*. Durham, NC: Duke University Press.

Yuval-Davis, Nira. 1997. *Gender and the Nation*. Thousand Oaks, CA: Sage Publications.

Index